THEY'RE
ALL
WHITE
JACK!

APARTHEID
ISN'T
CRICKET

NO PARKING

T0307399

Also available at all good book stores

9781785318252

9781785319952

9781785318191

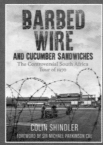

9781785316340

9781785315329

9781908051929

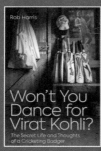

9781785317798

9781785317330

9781785317644

THE
TROUBLED
TOUR

DAVID POTTER

THE
TROUBLED
TOUR

South Africa in England 1960

First published by Pitch Publishing, 2022

Pitch Publishing
9 Donnington Park,
85 Birdham Road,
Chichester,
West Sussex,
PO20 7AJ
www.pitchpublishing.co.uk
info@pitchpublishing.co.uk

A CIP catalogue record is available for this book
from the British Library.

ISBN 978 1 80150 200 9

Typesetting and origination by Pitch Publishing
Printed and bound in India by Replika Press Pvt. Ltd.

Contents

INTRODUCTION

THERE ARE probably three reasons which impel me to revisit the South African tour of 1960: one political, one cricketing and one personal.

The political one is the obvious one of apartheid, for 1960 was the year in which the world – and not only the cricketing world – began to wake up to the horrors, injustice, cruelty and sheer waste of the apartheid system. If we did not know what it meant before 1960, we did so afterwards, and for the rest of the century, this word would haunt humanity. It really put cricket-lovers in a difficult position. So often have I looked at pictures of men like Jackie McGlew, Geoff Griffin, Colin Wesley and others and said, 'How could they possibly support a system like that?' I claim an excuse in 1960 for I was

7

only 11 and loved cricket. And yet, there were so many people, old enough to know better, who just shrugged their shoulders and said, 'It's nothing to do with us,' and worse still, 'Keep politics out of sport.' Such people must have loved the Berlin Olympics in 1936!

The cricketing reason is that I want to examine just why South Africa with so many potentially good players on board – McLean, Adcock and Waite would have been at least in the frame for a World XI – failed so badly against England. The reasons are obvious – one was that England were also good (and better) with two very fine fast bowlers, good leadership and a host of good batsmen, whereas the Springboks were hamstrung with the loss of one of their fast bowlers in a throwing controversy to which there was a little more, perhaps, than meets the eye. It was not entirely to do with Geoff Griffin. It had its genesis in Australia some 18 months previously, and had its repercussions and reverberations for many years to come. The English authorities and the umpires emerge with very little credit, but so too do the South Africans for failing to address the issue at an earlier stage, thus leaving themselves one fast bowler short.

And the personal one was that it was the series which hooked me on cricket, a passionate love affair which has now lasted 60 years and more. And yet I never saw in the flesh a single game. I celebrated my 12th birthday more or less at the end of that tour, and I lived in a small Scottish town many miles away from the action. Yet I followed it avidly. The year before the tour, our family had acquired a TV and this was the main conduit, but because the TV took up a lot of room, the radio had to be displaced and my mother allowed me to keep the now redundant radio (or 'the wireless' as it was called in 1960) in my room, effectively giving me exclusive access to the ball-by-ball radio coverage when the matches weren't on the telly. I was also able to go to the local reading room in the library where I was able to enjoy the *Manchester Guardian* and the *Daily Telegraph*, neither of which had as yet made much of an appearance in my Scottish working-class house.

One was more vitriolic about the system called apartheid than the other. This was the *Guardian* but it seemed always to have a major problem with misprints, so much so that it was often called the *Grauniad* in satirical magazines, which had little respect for the newly discovered condition called dyslexia! One can imagine the problems that it had with spelling 'apartheid'! In the *Daily Telegraph* newspaper, it was never all that difficult to detect a bias against northern counties and the Labour Party, both of which, to be fair, gave them loads of ammunition. However, both newspapers had a very large page about cricket, even county games, and were eagerly devoured by me even though I did not as yet have a great understanding of some of the terms. Not that it stopped me, however. I came home talking knowledgeably about 'deep cover point' 'silly mid-offs' 'leg traps' and 'drag', hoping that I was impressing everyone.

Previously I had watched a little cricket on the primitive television sets of my granny and some friends. I was too young to watch the Ashes of 1953 and had no real recollection of the previous South African tour of 1955, although I still have vivid and nightmarish recollections of football matches like Scotland 0 Uruguay 7 in the 1954 World Cup, soon after West Bromwich Albion 3 Preston North End 2 in the 1954 English FA Cup Final, and then Celtic 1 Clyde 1 in the 1955 Scottish Cup Final. But I did see a bit of the Laker Test match in 1956 (but not when the wickets were tumbling), a lot of the somewhat boring May and Cowdrey stand of 411, and more of the one-sided New Zealand tour of 1958. Our TV arrived on the Monday before the start of the final Test match against India in 1959, but that series too was one-sided, only intermittently interesting, and by then the football season had started.

1960 was the year that I first really developed an interest (an 'obsession' my mother said) in cricket, and I am grateful to Jackie McGlew's South Africans whom I, not really understanding apartheid, to my eternal shame supported. I always have had a soft spot for lost causes, and I did believe (and still do) that in some respects the South Africans got a rough deal in 1960. Besides, being Scottish, I sometimes found it difficult to support England! And that was before the horrendous 9-3 game at Wembley in 1961!

CHAPTER ONE

CRICKET IN 1960

'BASICALLY HEALTHY but in need of a tonic' is possibly the way that a doctor might have described cricket in England as the 1950s yielded to the new decade. One could argue when exactly football took over as the country's national game – some say England's World Cup triumph of 1966, some say earlier than that – but the truth of the matter was that the two sports were not really in competition in 1960. You could even play in both. 'Would Denis and Leslie Compton play for Arsenal or Middlesex?' was an argument for only the brief few weeks when the seasons overlapped. Normally cricket started at the end of April and stopped at the beginning of September; football had the FA Cup Final in early May and began again in late August. The two seasons yielded gracefully to each other, complemented each other and were both all the stronger for it.

There was no distinction between red-ball and white-ball cricket, simply because there was no white-ball cricket. The white ball was many decades in the future, and even the idea of limited-overs cricket, although not unknown, indeed flourishing in some areas at local level, was a distant concept for the future as far as the professional game was concerned, possibly something to do with the 'brighter cricket' that everyone kept talking about.

There were other differences as well. No player at any level would ever dream of wearing 'pyjamas'. Everything was white. Batsmen wore pads, gloves and the 'abdominal protector', but any thigh guards, elbow protector, etc. would be looked upon as the height of pretentiousness or even cowardice. On the head, a cap was worn. Even sunhats were still in the future, and it would be another 20 years before helmets began to make their appearance. All this meant that the task of a scorer and a spectator was a lot easier, for one could very quickly identify which batsman was which. It is not so easy today.

Test matches were the thing that brightened up the season, but the basic diet was the County Championship, won repeatedly throughout the 1950s by Surrey but won back by Yorkshire in 1959, and they would win it this year as well. All games were of three days' duration, beginning rigidly on a Saturday and a Wednesday with no play at all on Sunday, even though that Sabbatarian edifice had begun to crack at local level and many clubs played happily on a Sunday without any real apparent disapproval from God or that even more terrifying and influential character called the Archbishop of Canterbury. He was still able to decide who the Royal Family could marry but seemed less and less able to tell anyone else what to do. He was singularly failing to stop alcohol, sex and cricket on a Sunday, although professional cricket was slow to spot the opportunities.

Everyone seemed to moan about the County Championship. There were 17 counties, so if every county played every other county twice, that would be 32 games which was manageable and sensible. But now, if a county wanted to, it need only play 28 games, which meant 16 teams once and 12 of them twice. This seemed strange and unfair, and it meant that if you had a good match secretary you could end up avoiding Surrey and Yorkshire at least once!

There was a terrible predictability about the three-day game. County A would bat for all the first day, then declare about 6pm and hope to at least split the openers of the opposition before 6.30 when stumps were drawn. County B would then hope to bat until tea time on day two. County A would then bat again, and declare sometime on the last day, setting County B a target of something like 250 runs in 200 minutes. Overs did not come into it. Time-wasting was common.

There was never enough money – a *cri de cœur* which failed to resonate too loudly in the ears of the spectators who would have been very happy to play cricket for a living and a few days in a hotel on away fixtures. There was an awful lot of travelling. That was possibly true sometimes, and, certainly, in 1960 neither cars nor roads were as good as they are now, but half the games were at home and many of the away fixtures were not really all that far away – Worcestershire travelling to Warwickshire, or Lancashire travelling to Derbyshire were journeys that were by no means impossible or even all that difficult, but there were several crazy Tuesday or Friday nights when a county finished at Taunton at 5.30pm and had to be at Scarborough, all bright-eyed and bushy-tailed, for 11am the following morning.

There does seem to be a clear dichotomy of opinion about Sundays away from home. There were those who described it as a 'wonderful' day with a lovely hotel, golf tournaments, a big Sunday lunch, a visit to the bar on the Sunday afternoon followed by a walk around town, visiting beaches, castles, museums, etc. – whatever that town had to offer. Then at night a phone call home to the beautiful, dutiful and adoring wife and happy lisping children with details about losing a tooth and winning a prize at school.

That was a rosy, almost idyllic picture of a cricketer on an away Sunday. The reality was possibly different. It was more about team-mates getting on one's nerves, a hangover, the consequences of a foolish sexual misadventure the night before perhaps, rain and fretting about form and losing one's place in the team, not to mention the problems involved in having to share a room with a man who broke wind or moaned about himself when you were wanting to go to sleep. Or indeed having to share a meal with the man who had run you out the day before, or the captain who had dropped you from the side last week. And the mood of the company usually depended on how well the team were doing!

These trips did not happen every weekend, however, in fact possibly only about two or three times per season, and most spectators would have gladly put up with that occasional discomfort in return for the life of a professional cricketer. Ah, but there was the rub. Not everyone in 1960 was a professional cricketer. There were a few who were amateurs, men with their own private income who could play for nothing, even though it was hardly the world's best-kept secret that some 'amateurs' earned more than most professionals.

It was sometimes a murky business and owed its origins to nothing other than sheer snobbery. Grounds still had separate dressing rooms for amateurs and professionals (which meant four dressing rooms in each pavilion, presumably!); there were even, at some grounds, separate gates. There was an annual fixture between the Gentlemen (the amateurs) and the Players (the professionals) at Lord's and often repeated at Scarborough or some other festival in September. On away trips, professionals and amateurs usually stayed in separate hotels and there were no prizes awarded for guessing which group lived in the swankier hotel.

To modern eyes this is absolutely appalling, beyond comprehension even. It was much mocked and ridiculed in Australia, for example, and even the Labour Party in Great Britain was belatedly beginning to ask questions about it. And perhaps it is even valid to see the apartheid system which obtained in South Africa in this context. The class divide in Britain was possibly less rigid and certainly not imposed by violence or repression, but it was just as real in the minds of some people, with journalists like EW Swanton finding it hard to conceal his admiration for the gentleman amateur or 'chap', and who once tried to defend the infamous Lord Hawke who prayed to God that 'no professional would ever captain England'! The distinction was eventually done away with, to the chagrin of some at

Lord's, in 1963 when 'gentlemen' and 'players' all became 'cricketers'. The edifice had been cracking for some time, however, for Len Hutton had several years previously defied Lord Hawke's prayers by captaining England as a professional!

For professionals, there was something called a 'benefit' – more so than now. This too was much moaned about in books and magazines, for it involved a lot of turning up at events, and running raffles – again something that did not seem to some people to be absolutely out of the question. In return for this, a few youngsters and volunteers would go round the crowds asking spectators to contribute a few coins in a bucket. Some claimed that it was 'demeaning', but no player seemed reluctant to take the money! It was one of the traditions of the game, and to be fair, the life of a professional cricketer did not always seem to be a smart career option with two major disadvantages. How, for example, did one keep body and soul together in the winter? And what did one do when one got too old to play cricket?

So, to what extent was Britain a class-ridden society in 1960? Did cricket merely mirror society? Certainly, there had been a distinct air of patrician exclusivity about the Conservative Prime Ministers of that time. Winston Churchill 1951–1955, Anthony Eden 1955–1957 and Harold Macmillan 1957–1963 were no one's idea of a 'working man making good'! And yet they were benign aristocrats, or at least Churchill and Macmillan were, in that they had made no attempts to dismantle Labour's National Health Service and Welfare State. No one really knew about Eden for he decided to blow it all in 1956 on a mad military venture which history calls the Suez Crisis, but generally speaking, the Conservatives seemed to realise that the way to keep the lower orders in check was to treat them reasonably well. They deserve a great deal of credit for that.

Incidentally, in 1963, a few years after the events we are talking about, Lord Home became Sir Alec Douglas-Home in order to become Prime Minister and take a seat in the House of Commons. And he was the first Prime Minister who had ever played first-class cricket. He had played for Middlesex in the 1920s.

But perhaps as illuminating as anything in 1960 was the famous, thrilling, exciting, titillating but ultimately disappointing court case about DH Lawrence and a novel called *Lady Chatterley's Lover*. It seemed to be all about sex, but in fact it was as much about social class as anything else. The book had first been published privately in 1928, but had led a distinctly low-profile existence in this country until Penguin published it in 1960 and it soon sold three million copies when word got around that it had been banned in other countries. Very soon, it got another undeserved boost when someone tried to get it banned in Great Britain as well!

The court case happened in autumn 1960, not long after the South Africans had gone home, but it was indicative of several traits of British society. In the first place, it revealed the perennial love of prurient, voyeuristic sexuality, but that is hardly surprising. Indeed, it is a necessary part of the human condition. Another was the British love of litigation, and yet another was the British obsession with social class. Lady Chatterley's husband had been wounded and disabled in the Great War and unable to perform the basic and obvious function for his wife. Still loving, but increasingly frustrated, the good Lady formed a relationship, not with another man of her own class (which would have been bad enough but understandable and even forgivable), but (shock! horror!) with her gamekeeper who did the necessary in his hut in the woods with a relentless ferocity to the delight of both parties – and to all those who read the book, the sales of which naturally rose as quickly and as regularly as the gamekeeper's member.

By modern standards, perhaps, the descriptions of the coupling were tame and often wrapped in metaphorical and figurative language, even though the 'f' word made an appearance now and again. But what really upset a few people was the class aspect of all this. A gamekeeper! Had he played cricket, he would have been a professional. He should have known his place, which was certainly not between the thighs of his employer's wife. And there was the notorious comment of the prosecuting counsel who asked the question (apparently genuinely and without any tongue in cheek or sarcasm) if this was a book which you would want your wife or your servants [sic] to read!

It was astonishing. Even in 1960, having servants was not common. Most of the working classes now worked in factories and offices, but here we had a Colonel Blimp (or whatever the legal equivalent was) asking a fatuous question like that! In any case, the jury decided that Lady C (as she was called) was not obscene. So perhaps social class was still there, but possibly decreasing in its importance. Or was it?

In general terms, one would have to say that things in Great Britain were prospering. The country had recovered remarkably well from the Second World War which was now a receding memory. Unemployment had virtually gone, prosperity was in the air, new houses had been built and were continuing to be built, working-class families now were beginning to aspire to owning televisions, cars and even taking foreign holidays. The Conservatives, having ditched Eden for his absurd and dangerous Suez adventure of 1956, had fought back to win the General Election of October 1959 under Harold Macmillan, who loved being quoted as saying, 'We've never had it so good.' And he was right. It was as if the penny had at last dropped that the best way to keep the rebellious lower orders in check was not by poverty, unemployment, repressive religion and bogus guilt-ridden patriotism, but by jobs, good houses, a national health service and by entertainment and sport.

'*Panem et circenses*' (bread and circuses) said Juvenal in Ancient Rome in the context of keeping the urban mob happy. Macmillan seemed to agree.

In cricket, at international level, England had, with one painful exception, defeated everyone in recent years. At home Jim Laker had spun out the Australians in 1956, the West Indians had been beaten in 1957 in a series much remembered for the 411-stand of May and Cowdrey at Edgbaston, a partnership which combined resolute defiance with astonishing tedium, and the series of 1958 against New Zealand and of 1959 against India had been embarrassing mismatches. South Africa had last been in England in 1955 and England had won 3-2.

Abroad, England had drawn 2-2 with South Africa in 1956/57 and recently they had come home from the West Indies with a narrow and not always exciting 1-0 win. But there was one hurtful fly in the ointment and that had been in 1958/59 when they had lost the Ashes comprehensively to Australia, 4-1. This had hurt, and more printers' ink had been spilled on that one unhappy tour than on all the series they had won. And there was one particular aspect of that tour which would very much be alive when South Africa came calling in 1960.

England did not usually boast. They were usually good winners and that was when we tended to hear patronising words like 'sportsmanship' and phrases like 'the best man won' and 'gallant losers' to cheer up the colonials who had been less successful. England winning was more or less what one would expect, and it was almost as if that was what was meant to happen. It was like the Conservatives winning a General Election, everyone reading about it in the *Daily Telegraph* and then going to the Church of England to sing 'Now Thank We All Our God'. The novelist RF Delderfield wrote a series of books called *God Is an Englishman*. The title was obviously sarcastic, but one wonders whether there were some people who actually believed that!

It was a different matter when England lost. They whinged. The Ashes defeats of 1946/47 and of 1950/51 could be explained away, somehow or other, by the difficult problems of recovering from a world war when a Labour Government was in power, but 1954/55 had seen Len Hutton and Frank Tyson bring the Ashes home, and hopes had been high in 1958 as the team sailed away with the accompaniment of the normal 'best team ever to leave these shores'. But from the moment that Jack Fingleton began his report on the radio on that cold morning of 5 December 1958 with the words: 'Hello England, I have bad news for you, which of course is good news for us...' before telling us that England were all out for a miserable 134 in Brisbane, it was clear that England were struggling.

There are usually many excuses that one can put forward for an Ashes defeat – injuries, illnesses, homesickness, umpires, dropped catches, pitches being 'doctored' by the Australians and bad luck with the toss spring to mind. But on this occasion there was another one and that was the bowling action of Ian Meckiff and, to a lesser extent, Gordon Rorke, who were accused of throwing. Spearheaded by the redoubtable EW Swanton, who was pompous and opinionated but never really a hard-hitting, money-driven, investigative journalist, the press handed the English public back home a reason for England's defeat. The throwing was 'blatant', according to EWS. But the rest of the world wondered if it would have been quite so blatant had the perpetrator been a Home Counties Englishman.

Such a simplistic assessment of 'chucking' ignored at least three other factors. One was that Meckiff was born that way. He simply could not straighten his left bowling arm. Another was the excellence of other Australians like Richie Benaud, Norman O'Neill and Alan Davidson, and yet another was the incompetence and fatalistic attitude of so many of the England players who seemed to have decided as early as the first day of the first Test that the world was against them and that they were not going to win. 'Fighting back' was absent from the mindset of so many England players, and the somewhat aristocratic and out of touch leadership of PBH May was not able to jog them out of it. It was, simply, an awful tour. And it hurt.

What did not help was that May's fiancée appeared on the tour as well. This was the extremely well-connected Virginia Gilligan, daughter of previous captain Harold Gilligan. The rest of the party were not allowed to bring wives or girlfriends, so it was hardly a boost to morale for them to see the captain being allowed preferential treatment while everyone else was deprived of such basic needs! Trying to paper over the cracks of this rift, the England party could talk about the 'throwing' of the Australians to divert attention from internal divisions.

More relevantly to the 1960 South African tour, it meant that the spectre of 'chucking' would hang over English cricket for some time. Had England lost to the West Indies in the Caribbean in early 1960, one suspects that more might have been made of the bowling actions of some of the West Indies fast men, and the South African series of 1960 certainly took place in an atmosphere of cricketing paranoia about fast bowlers throwing the ball, rather than bowling it. When it became known that the South African party was to contain a fellow called Geoff Griffin who had been called twice for throwing in season 1958/59 (funnily enough, not 1959/60), you could almost smell the trouble that was coming.

The Australians were due back in England in 1961. It is possibly not entirely fanciful to suggest that 1960 was all about making sure that Meckiff was not chosen for 1961, and there was little doubt that 'chucking', fuelled by a malign combination of the MCC and the popular press, would feature largely in 1960. It was almost as if it was expected to happen – and funnily enough, it did. It is sometimes called 'fate' and 'destiny' but it is more likely to be the combination of so many wills, conscious and subconscious, which cause such things, and so many people simply get swept along in it all. There are fashions in cricket as there are in everything else. 'Chucking' was definitely 'in' in 1960.

In his basically and uncharacteristically gloomy prognosis of the 1960 season, John Arlott in *Cricket on Trial* identified four problems that cricket must address:

a. The impact of politics on the South African tour

b. The loss of public interest in the changing world of the affluent 1960s

c. The 'popular' press with all its 'revelations'

d. Chucking

The last one was highlighted even before the end of April in two separate and unrelated incidents, although one wonders whether there was already some subliminal influence on the umpires. On Wednesday, 27 April in the Surrey v Cambridge University game, spinner Tony Lock (who had also been called in the West Indies as early as 1953/54 and several times since) was called by umpire Arthur Fagg for throwing, and on Saturday, 30 April, on the very day that the South Africans played their first game at Arundel, John Aldridge of Worcestershire was called by Jack Crapp for the same offence in a game against Glamorgan at Pontypridd. Oddly enough, no one seemed to make any jokes along the lines of 'that was Crap(p)'.

CHAPTER TWO

SOUTH AFRICA IN 1960

IT IS probably true to say that in early 1960 people in Great Britain, as a general rule, knew little about South Africa and cared even less. Sixty years had now passed since the Boer War of 1899–1902 and since then South Africa had sided with Britain in two world wars and had generally been a loyal member of the Empire and then the Commonwealth. The word 'apartheid' was known but the opposition to it in Great Britain was remarkably slow to gather pace, mainly because the left was too involved in its own internecine arguments about nuclear disarmament and the nationalisation of industries. The South Africans themselves talked about 'separate development' (the word 'apartheid' was translated as 'apart hood') and they kept making patronising statements about how much they loved the black man and how they were protecting him from communism. This and other such humbug was sadly swallowed by quite a few politicians who should have known a lot better.

Indeed, on the surface, apartheid did not seem all that bad either. 'Separate development' sounded plausible. The black man had started from a different point compared with the white man; through no fault of their own, they had not had the benefit of Judaeo-Christian theology and ethics, nor Greco-Roman thought and literature, and it sounded only sensible that they should move at different paces. The trouble was that it was not like that at all. Basically, white people were rich, and black people poor. White people lived in lovely houses; black people lived in shanty towns, patronisingly called 'townships'. Black children, no matter how bright, would not be admitted to universities. The differences were enforced by a repressive police force.

And there were the obvious differences, petty and bizarre in some cases. There were things like park benches reserved for whites only, for example. One would like to hear some sort of rationale for this. How could this be defended? Did they honestly believe that black people were more likely to pass on disease than white people were? Perhaps there was a fear that white men might fall in love with and, horror of horrors, have sexual relations with a black woman. Even worse was the possibility of it happening the other way round! One's daughter having a good time with a black man must have been one of the most horrendous nightmares of the white South African. Indeed, if that happened, it would have to be rape.

The Church did not seem to care, either in South Africa or Great Britain. Worse still, the Churches in South Africa, the Dutch Reformed Church in particular, were all in favour, and of course unscrupulous clerics will find in the Old Testament plenty of material to take out of context and to weld into some bogus political point to justify their system. Churches throughout history have always been able to justify anything. For centuries, churches in England, Scotland and Rome saw nothing wrong with slavery!

In 1960, some Churches in Great Britain, did, to their credit, begin to question some of what was going on, but it was far too easy to sweep everything to one side and to say 'let those who live there and who know what they are talking about solve the problem'. There were honourable exceptions like Reverend David Sheppard, who had played Test cricket for England, for example, but generally the patronising idea of 'mission' was a strong one. White people had the job of educating the black people, it was said. The South Africans, by their kind, beneficial and helpful policies towards the natives, were doing just that. It was to the benefit of everyone, the gullible were led to believe. It was sometimes called, astonishingly, 'the white man's burden'.

I was brought up in the Church of Scotland. Every week for Sunday School I had to take a threepenny piece for the offering 'for all the little black boys and girls'. On the wall was a picture about Mission. It was a subliminal version of the Last Supper. About 12 well-clad, well-fed black boys were looking and smiling gratefully and respectfully at the white man in his dog collar giving his exegesis of a miracle or two while Christ on the cross hovered up above. And I was told that my threepence was going towards all that. It wouldn't have been so bad if it were true. In fact, as I later discovered, a lot of the threepenny pieces went towards church administration and clerical salaries in Edinburgh!

The Prime Minister of Great Britain Harold Macmillan was not one of these naïve people. He realised that change had to come in Africa and that former British colonies in Africa would have to have their freedom, otherwise there might be a bloodbath. Following a tour of these colonies, on 3 February 1960, Macmillan delivered before both Houses of the South African Parliament his famous 'Wind of Change' (sometimes later called the 'Winds of Change') speech in which he made it clear that he would not stand in the way of black nations getting their freedom, and he included South Africa in his comments, saying that, 'As a fellow member of the Commonwealth, it is our earnest desire to give South Africa our support and encouragement, but I hope you won't mind my saying frankly that there are some aspects of your policies which make it impossible for us to do this without being false to our own deep convictions about the political destinies of free men to which in our own territories we are trying to give effect.'

The speech was greeted with stony silence. His own right-wingers looked upon it as a betrayal of Conservative values, but he was only moving with the times. He was far more astute than most politicians of the time on this issue, but it was looked upon in South Africa as a threat, and this iconic speech would, in time, play its part in South Africa's withdrawal from the Commonwealth. It was a timely warning, sadly ignored.

Events were now moving in that direction very quickly in any case, and little more than a month after Macmillan's visionary speech, the world saw just exactly what apartheid was all about. In what history now calls the Sharpeville Massacre, some 250 black people were gunned down by the South African police for protesting against 'pass laws', the 'pass laws' in themselves being a gross infringement of human rights, and involving the need for some kind of control of movement. The massacre happened on 21 March 1960, about a month before the South African cricketers were to leave for Great Britain. Some crass South African politicians stated that there was a link here, and that Macmillan, by his famous speech, had in fact encouraged an insurrection! They also talked about the need to keep law and order, and mentioned 'communist subversives' who had been infiltrated from Russia. Harold Macmillan was hardly a 'communist subversive'! Sadly, some people seemed to believe that he was!

So where did all this leave the South African cricketers? It is hard to believe that men like Jackie McGlew and Neil Adcock, who would prove themselves to be such charming visitors later on in the summer, could possibly be in favour of Sharpeville. Even though they may have supported the general policy of apartheid (in fact it seemed that they did), they cannot really have been in favour of such violence. Could they? Yet in some ways the cricketers themselves were the victims of their own system in that they could hardly be expected to condemn their own government while in another country. It was not like, for example, a Labour sympathiser criticising, say, the pay policy of the Conservatives. It was far more basic than that. They were in the same position as non-Nazi Germans were in the 1930s. They could hardly speak out against this outrage, but, by saying nothing, did they not seem to be acquiescing and even supporting their evil regime?

There was little doubt that the South African cricketers owed their high standard of living and even their ability to play cricket to apartheid. Cricket and rugby were undeniably the sports of the rich white settlers. Black people, as a rule, did not play cricket. There were two reasons for this – one is that they lacked the facilities, and the other was they were not encouraged to do so. It was sadly part of apartheid that black boys played football, rather than any other sport. All football really needed was a football. Cricket, at any level other than street cricket with a rubber ball and a piece of wood, required sophisticated and expensive equipment. It also usually pre-supposed a certain level of teaching and coaching about the game.

And yet why was it that South African cricketers did not wonder why the only countries they could play against were England, Australia and New Zealand? They were not likely to play against the West Indies, India and Pakistan. Did they never express any desire to play against Gary Sobers and Rohan Kanhai? Were they so acculturated into their own evil system? Did they not realise that Harold Macmillan was trying to tell them something? Did they not realise that by opening the doors of their cricket clubs to black children who were such a large section of their population, they would actually strengthen their sport and their country?

John Waite, the South African wicketkeeper, wrote a book, along with his collaborator Dick Whitington, about the tour, called *Perchance to Bowl*. It is a fascinating account of the tour with many nuggets of information from the inside, as it were. The book contains a chapter called 'Why White Cricketers Do Not Play Non-White Cricketers in South Africa'. It is a fascinating read written by a clearly intelligent man who is tasked with defending the indefensible. He is reduced to attacking the Reverend David Sheppard who was opposed to apartheid and 'we did wonder whether he had forgotten the attitude Jesus Christ adopted in regard to Mary Magdalene on the occasion of their original meeting' – the theological significance of which, I must confess, escapes me. And how patronising is this? 'The South African native, in his opinion [that of Waite's collaborator Dick Whitington] has all the good points of a child, and if treated with the love and discipline that parents expend upon children, will remain as loyal and loving to his "mastah" as well-raised children remain to their parents.' It is like a breeder of pedigree dogs recommending his latest breed to his customer. The other Dick Whitington – or Whittington, in fact – is a sometime pantomime character. This one has all the hallmarks of a clown.

At another point, 'He [Mr Whitington] realizes, as the outside world still seems unable to realize, that three million whites cannot keep 12 million non-whites in luxury or anything approaching luxury.' One would like to think that Waite, an excellent wicketkeeper, batsman and cricket writer, has his tongue in his cheek at this point, and is having us on. Sadly, he is not.

Clearly if Waite's attitude was typical – and one suspects that it was in 1960 – there were very few points of contact between South Africa and the rest of the world, and it was little wonder that the 1960 tour met with demonstrations. Fortunately for cricket, demonstrations with placards and pamphlets were as far as they got at this stage, and the tour went ahead. Now and again, one heard of threats to pour oil over wickets and damage pitches, but fortunately that didn't happen, and the cricket went ahead.

And yet, might it not have been better if the 1960 tour, in the wake of the awful events of Sharpeville, had indeed been aborted? Might it not have led to an earlier realisation that South Africa was out of step with the rest of the world, and that a few steps in a more liberal direction might have paid dividends?

The words of South African journalist Charles Fortune in his book *Cricket Overthrown* are illuminating. 'For weeks before the South African team set off, our newspapers in the Union had carried stories of the opposition rife in England to the visit of the Springboks. Priests and politicians, scholars and undergraduates had, it seemed, gone on record and into action in an all-out attempt to stop the cricket tour before it set out from Johannesburg. Through all this sound and fury, the Marylebone Cricket Club had kept its composure, sure that the anti-tour move and the support this move received from the more left-wing of the London morning papers, failed completely to reflect the basic English attitude. So quickly did it prove. What demonstration there was turned out to be a sad little affair: no organization, hackneyed, no dignity. There is in South Africa a women's organization that for some years staged its silent demonstration against the government in South Africa every time any cabinet minister set foot out of doors. If the English churches and the English press truly had felt some need to express disapproval of matters South African on the occasion of the Springboks visit, then these all-powerful organizations might have translated their utterances into some positive action. Instead, only a tattered and bleak little conglomeration of chilly-looking adolescents turned out to show and to voice their objection to the arrival in England of the South African cricket team. Inevitably the impression was created that these demonstrations were no more than the cats-paws of certain churchmen who had seized on the visit of the cricketers as an opportunity to gain for themselves some public notice: that some newspapers had at the same time found in the occasion an opportunity for cheap headlines gleaned on the cheap. As MCC had so rightly discerned, England en masse would have none of it.'

This quote clearly written from a South African perspective and almost triumphalist in tone, does, however, highlight the rather important point that the demonstrations were sadly sporadic and disorganised in character. There was as yet no co-ordinated leadership, no strong organisation to oppose apartheid. The Church of England, as a body, resolutely failed to come out against the South African method of government. There were exceptions, notably Reverend David Sheppard, and there were a few clerics who would pray for better understanding between the races in South Africa, but universal condemnation came there none. As a result, it was easy for the *Daily Telegraph*, for example, to ridicule the protesters as 'beatniks' and 'weirdos' who would have been better employed getting a job or studying for their exams.

A year or two earlier, a similar thing had happened with the nuclear disarmament people. Because they lacked the 'respectable' support of a Church, they were easily portrayed as the hairy, the unwashed, the sexually degenerate and even to be ridiculed. 'More to be pitied than laughed at,' was a favourite right-wing phrase to describe the idealistic young. They could be exposed as being manipulated by agents paid by Moscow! It would take a few years – but it would happen in the late 1960s – for nuclear disarmament, anti-apartheid and indeed the anti-Vietnam war movement from 1964 onwards to become 'respectable'. It is now recognised that each one of these three 'causes' is a correct one. But it wasn't in 1960.

'Keep politics out of sport' was the cry of the apartheid appeasers. It was specious and superficially attractive. 'Here we are, trying to play cricket,' they claimed, 'and these protesters are trying to stop us.' Words like 'freedom' and 'fair play' were bandied about. In the same way as an Englishman's home was his castle, so too was his cricket field his demesne. But sportsmen have responsibilities to decency and justice as well. Trouble is that when you are 11 years old, you don't really understand all that, and cricket is cricket. To my shame – and I have regretted this many times in my later life – I began to support the South Africans of 1960. I did wonder about apartheid, however!

CHAPTER THREE

ARRIVAL AND ACCLIMATISATION

THE 15 players who flew in to London on Sunday, 17 April 1960 were as follows:

DJ McGlew – captain (Natal) 24 caps, age 31, right-handed batsman

TL Goddard – vice captain (Natal) 15 caps, age 28, left-handed batsman, left-armed bowler

NAT Adcock – (Natal) 19 caps, age 29, fast bowler

PR Carlstein – (Transvaal) 1 cap, age 21, right-handed batsman and occasional leg-spinner

CAR Duckworth – (Rhodesia) 2 caps, age 27, deputy wicketkeeper

JP Fellows-Smith – (Transvaal) uncapped, age 28, all-rounder

G Griffin – (Natal) uncapped, age 20, fast bowler

AH McKinnon – (Eastern Province), uncapped, age 27, left-armed spin bowler

RA McLean – (Natal) 28 caps, age 29, right-handed batsman, generally looked upon as their best batsman

S O'Linn – (Transvaal) uncapped, age 32, left-handed batsman, already known to the English public because he had played cricket for Kent and football for Charlton Athletic

AJ Pithey – (Rhodesia) 3 caps, age 23, right-handed batsman

JE Pothecary – (Western Province) uncapped, age 26, right-armed fast bowler

HJ Tayfield – (Natal) 32 caps, age 30, very experienced off-spinner

JHB Waite – (Transvaal) 31 caps, age 31, wicketkeeper

C Wesley – (Natal) uncapped, age 22, left-handed batsman, left-armed bowler

Dudley Nourse – manager

Seven of these players – McGlew, McLean, Waite, Tayfield, Duckworth, Goddard and Adcock had been in England in 1955, and of these seven, the first named four had toured in 1951 as well, although Tayfield was a late substitute that year. There were now no 'survivors' from 1947. There were six uncapped players.

Possibly the only surprise for English cricket fans was the non-selection of hostile fast bowler Peter Heine who had in the past formed a very strong opening partnership with Neil Adcock. He had taken five wickets in his debut in 1955 and had generally been very impressive, but the South African selectors had chosen Geoff Griffin as Adcock's partner.

It was a decision that they would regret. Heine had been a little wayward on occasion, but he was still a fine bowler, and it was felt that he had at least one good tour left in him. His name would keep recurring in cricketing conversations over the summer!

The recent South African season had seen Natal win the Currie Cup. The 1961 *Wisden* perhaps tells us something about the perception of South African cricket in England at the time. In the section 'Overseas Cricket' (the name perhaps in itself an indication of imperialist paternalism), the Australian 1959/60 season is well reported with full scorecards and reports of all Sheffield Shield games and has 22 pages devoted to it, whereas the South African season has brief 'potted' scorecards and is given only three and a half pages.

The Currie Cup Section A consisted of Natal, Transvaal, Western Province, Rhodesia and Border, whereas Section B had Transvaal B, Eastern Province, Orange Free State, North-Eastern Transvaal and Griqualand West. One would have thought that teams might have played each other twice to make eight games, or once to make four, but both sections, bafflingly, played six games.

Jackie McGlew apparently had not been in the best of health and suffered intermittently from a bad back, but

Trevor Goddard and Roy McLean had both had good seasons with the bat, and Geoff Griffin had done well with the ball, taking, for example, 7-36 and then 4-22 for Natal against Western Province and 5-49 against Rhodesia. He had also had a few good scores with the bat, and had not, apparently, been called for a no-ball all season, although he had, on a couple of occasions, the season before. On the down side, Border had been dismissed for 16 and 18 when playing against Natal. There had been two Test trial games in February but they had been devastated by rain, and the closest that South Africa came to international cricket was a tour of Denis Compton's Commonwealth XI in October and November 1959 which *Wisden* tells us was 'not a money-spinner'. It contained men like Brian Close and Bobby Simpson, and even Roy Marshall of the West Indies. Sadly, Marshall was the exception that proved the rule. He was white, and the son of a wealthy plantation owner.

Natal's success meant that seven of their players were selected for the tour. Only one player, Atholl McKinnon of Eastern Province, was chosen from a Section B side. It was looked upon as a strong, if slightly inexperienced and unproven side, although everyone was aware that England at home would be very hard to beat. Presciently, however, *Wisden 1960* states that: 'If the South Africans can increase the tempo of their batting, they will be welcomed wherever they go, but, like most other countries, they now find that their safety-first methods of the past have left a dearth of stroke-makers.' Indeed, the only proven stroke-maker of the Springbok side was Roy McLean.

Wisden 1960 looked forward to the tour, pointing out that this was the ninth South African team to visit Great Britain since PW Sherwell brought the first team here in 1907. They had won only one series and that was in 1935 when HF Wade's team did the job. Recent series had been close – 3-2 for England in 1955, and 2-2 in South Africa in 1956/57. But South Africa had not played a Test match since the winter of 1957/58 when they had gone down 3-0 to the Australians. In England, 36 Test matches had been played against South Africa, and South Africa had won only four, one in 1935, one in 1951 and two in 1955. But South Africa had improved and 1960 was expected to be close.

There were still a few cricketing fans who recalled their first visit in 1907 and their great spin bowlers of that year – Bert Vogler, Reggie Schwarz, Aubrey Faulkner and Gordon White. Clearly, they had made a great impression. RE Forster writing in *Wisden 1908* says that 1907 will be remembered for two things – the appalling weather and the excellence of the South African spinners, all of whom bowled googlies, 'bosies' or 'wrong uns', i.e. bowling with a leg break action but persuading the ball to come in to the right-handed batsman rather than go away from him. The 'proud originator' of this style of bowling, *Wisden* tells us, was the Englishman Bosanquet who mesmerised the Australians with it, but then he taught Reggie Schwarz who taught the others. Bert Vogler was the best, however, according to *Wisden*.

The 1960 programme had been arranged and negotiated well in advance, and the modern reader is immediately struck by several things. One is the obvious absence of any one-day internationals, which were still a good decade and more in the future. Another is that there were no trips to either Scotland or Ireland, which was a shame to the many devotees of the sport in both countries, while there were two trips to Wales to play Glamorgan in Cardiff and Swansea. Every other county had a three-day game with the tourists – a much-looked-forward-to occasion and usually a money-spinner. Both Oxford and Cambridge University had a game against the South Africans, and games started rigidly every Wednesday and Saturday except Test matches, which began on a Thursday to allow for a day's practice on the Wednesday after the England players had arrived from their Tuesday commitment with their various counties. Normally there were six Test grounds in England for five Test matches. This year it was Headingley in Leeds that was the unlucky ground. The tour began and ended with a few 'Mickey Mouse' fixtures which were quaint anachronisms but still in 1960 looked upon as very much part of the English cricket scene.

April 30 – Duke of Norfolk's XI	Arundel
May 4, 5, 6 – Worcestershire	Worcester
May 7, 9, 10 – Derbyshire	Derby
May 11, 12, 13 – Oxford University	Oxford
May 14, 16, 17 – Essex	Ilford
May 18, 19, 20 – Cambridge University	Cambridge
May 21, 23, 24 – MCC	Lord's

May 25, 26, 27 – Northamptonshire   Northampton

May 28, 30, 31 – Nottinghamshire   Trent Bridge

June 1, 2, 3 – Minor Counties   Stoke-on-Trent

June 4, 6, 7 – Glamorgan   Cardiff

June 9, 10, 11, 13, 14 ENGLAND FIRST TEST

Edgbaston

June 15, 16, 17 – Somerset   Taunton

June 18, 20, 21 – Hampshire   Southampton

June 23, 24, 25, 27, 28 ENGLAND SECOND TEST

Lord's

June 29, 30, July 1 – Gloucestershire   Bristol

July 2, 4, 5 – Lancashire   Old Trafford

July 7, 8, 9, 11, 12 ENGLAND THIRD TEST

Trent Bridge

July 13, 14, 15 –Leicestershire   Leicester

July 16, 18, 19 – Middlesex   Lord's

July 21, 22, 23, 25, 26 ENGLAND FOURTH TEST

Old Trafford

July 27, 28, 29 – Surrey   The Oval

July 30, August 1, 2 – Glamorgan   Swansea

August 3, 4, 5 – Warwickshire   Edgbaston

August 6, 8, 9 – Yorkshire   Sheffield

August 10, 11, 12 – Sussex   Hove

August 13, 15, 16 – Kent   Canterbury

August 18, 19, 20, 22, 23 ENGLAND FIFTH TEST

The Oval

August 27, 29, 30 – Combined Services   Portsmouth

August 30, 31, September 1 – AER Gilligan's XI

Hastings

September 3, 5, 6 – A Lancashire XI   Blackpool

September 7, 8, 9 – TN Pearce's XI   Scarborough

The 15 men practised at Lord's and they had a few games with youngsters. Their presence in London did not attract any great attention, apart from a harmless and peaceful demonstration when they arrived on 17 April. They then adjusted to weather, food and all the other differences that exist between different countries. The weather in April is not always conducive to cricket or even cricket practice: 1960 was no exception.

The tour began, as good tours did in those days, with a one-day, light-hearted, unofficial game in the grounds of Arundel Castle, West Sussex against the Duke of Norfolk's XI on 30 April. It gave cricket fans their first chance to see the South African tourists, many of whom were totally unfamiliar and on their first visit to the UK. It was a bright day, but generally agreed to be just a little on the cold side for watching cricket.

The Duke of Norfolk, a genuine cricket fan, had invited a few big names for his side – Roy Marshall of Hampshire, Freddie Titmus of Middlesex and a real golden oldie in Keith Miller of Australia, as well as some enthusiastic club cricketers of lesser ability. The Duke's team batted first and declared at 220/8. The best bowling came from Hugh Tayfield who took 5-102 with his off breaks, but Geoff Griffin also bowled, impressing spectators with his pace, but also already causing a few eyebrows to raise about his bowling action, which was very open-chested, and he did seem sometimes to bowl with a bent arm. There were rumours circulating that he had been 'called' a couple of times in South Africa, although not last season. These rumours were in fact true.

Charles Fortune, the South African journalist, in his book *Cricket Overthrown* tells the story of how as the match was nearing its end, Crawford White of the *News*

Chronicle approached him and said, 'Charles, your chap Griffin: I'm convinced he throws. What do you feel?' Fortune's reply was a masterpiece of question dodging while at the same time giving a plausible answer: 'What I feel isn't of any importance – but keep in mind he has not run foul of any South African umpire through the season just ended in the Union and Rhodesia. He has been accepted by our South African Board of Control and that Board went out of its way to proclaim that in no circumstances would it tolerate any bowler tainted with a thrower's delivery.'

When one reads between the lines, the implication of all that would be that Charles Fortune, if pressed, would possibly agree that there was something dodgy about Griffin's action. And it was already clear that the press were scenting a story here before the tour had properly started and on the basis of five overs sent down in a warm-up game.

The story would of course run for a long, long time and there was a great deal more to it than merely Griffin's bent arm. Things were boiling up quite nicely for the drama that was to come.

In reply, Jackie McGlew hit 72, and Roy McLean 54 against some mediocre bowling and fielding, as one would expect at the start of the season with the weather not really warm enough for cricket, and players still a little rusty. The South Africans won comfortably, but it mattered little. The tour would open properly on Wednesday at Worcester.

The game itself did not engender any great media reaction. *The People*, for example, a populist newspaper which brought sex, football and gossip to the masses, had little to say. A few quotes about how McKinnon might not be as good as he had been billed, but how Fellows-Smith and Griffin might cause England problems, but the back pages were more concerned with Burnley's imminent lifting of the league championship and the retirement of Tom Finney of Preston North End. In cricket Godfrey Evans told of a row he had with skipper Len Hutton on the 1953/54 tour of the West Indies when the players were told to avoid a social function on the night before a Test match, but Hutton himself went as guest of honour! Evans also told us, to no one's surprise really, that Hutton could not stand fellow Yorkshiremen, Jim Laker and Johnny

Wardle. Yorkshire cricketers were never famous for liking each other!

But the cricket season had not yet really got itself going.

CHAPTER FOUR

MAY

THE INITIAL first-class game of the tour was at Worcester, that lovely ground in the shadow of the cathedral where tours often start. The tourists arrived by train on the night of Tuesday, 2 May to a large police presence in the station to deal with any potential demonstration, but there were no demonstrators in sight. This indeed would be a pattern during this tour, that the fears of demonstrations were more than the demonstrations themselves. There were a few protests throughout the summer, but they were sporadic and there was no serious disruption to the cricket, something for which even left-wing-sympathising cricket lovers (and there were loads) were truly thankful. Such protesters as there were tended to be middle-aged, middle-class, people with a conscience, often Church people – not irresponsible anarchists.

The team were met at Worcester station by the mayor and duly travelled unmolested to their hotel. Worcester had been looking forward to this event, but there was unusual competition for attention. This was because on Friday, 6 May, the last day of the game, there was going to be a wedding in London – the royal wedding of Princess Margaret and Antony Armstrong Jones – and the whole occasion was on television. This may explain why the Worcestershire game was not televised (the first game of a tour often was) because this was 1960 and BBC resources were restricted!

Television in itself would have been a novelty for the South African tourists, for there was as yet no television network in South Africa, and they might have felt themselves to be privileged to be in the country at royal wedding time. But maybe not. The BBC made sure that those who love that sort of thing had loads of opportunities to say 'Ooh!' and 'Ah!' and 'Isn't she pretty!' but many people would have felt a little bored by it all. It was certainly the first royal wedding in which television had played such a huge, even dominating, part.

It was hardly the first or last royal wedding to be not quite what it seemed, but this one was particularly and spectacularly flawed. The Queen's only sister, Margaret was certainly nice-looking but had been thwarted in her matrimonial intentions in 1955 (the last time the South Africans had been here, incidentally) when her sister and the Archbishop of Canterbury had prevented her from marrying a decent fellow called Peter Townsend, who ticked a few of the right boxes, including a creditable war record, and wealth ... but was sadly divorced. 'No, no, we can't have that, Margaret,' and she was given a patronising lecture about 'duty' instead, with no doubt a stern reminder of how Uncle Eddy had let everyone down in 1936 when lusty feelings about Wallis Simpson got in the way of 'duty'.

It would be hard to believe that this blow put an end to Margaret's sexual adventures or misadventures, however – but could you really blame her? – and after a few years of sly innuendoes in the press, it was announced she was now going to marry a photographer called Antony Armstrong-

Jones. He looked OK, but he was a commoner, even though he was rich enough. The best man at the wedding had to be replaced. 'Jaundice' was given as the reason, but it transpired that the gentleman concerned had committed a 'minor offence' in Hyde Park – and everyone knew what that meant! It soon turned out that Antony himself was versatile in his affections, and Margaret too was no dutiful, chaste wife, soon earning the nickname of 'Mad Meg' for her sometimes blatant indiscretions on the island of Mustique. It all happened far away, but it did not escape the notice of our gossip columnists. All this seemed to be making a statement to her sister, as daughters-in-law and granddaughters-in-law would continue to do to the same lady in future years. In the long and lamentable catalogue of royal marriage failures, this one turned out to be a collector's item.

All in all, the good housewives of Worcester who tuned in to the TV that day would have been better going along to New Road. They would have seen some fine cricket, particularly from the South Africans as they finished off Worcestershire by 133 runs, the game ending, in any case, early enough on the Friday to allow people to see some of the royal wedding!

The first day, Wednesday, 4 May, had seen the South Africans bat all day to declare at 365/6. The day belonged to Roy McLean who hit 207, along with Tony Pithey, who scored a worthy 76 after the team had been reduced to 28/3 with Jack Flavell looking likely to rip through the Springboks. But McLean played magnificently with more or less every shot in the book and his innings contained 34 crisp fours played all over the ground. He was supported by Sid O'Linn and young Colin Wesley near the end, and eventually fell at cover point to Len Coldwell. But it was an excellent start to the tour, and showed that the South Africans had at least one top-class batsman in the hard-hitting McLean. Roy's problem, however, was not lack of class. It was lack of consistency. This 207 would, not surprisingly, turn out to be the highest score hit by any South African on the tour. McLean did score a century in the Test match at Old Trafford, but his tour average ended up as a slightly disappointing 37.9 and there were several key times when his team-mates might have expected more of him than they got.

Thursday saw South Africa in the field. Griffin was not playing and there were those who suggested that this may have been because Jack Crapp, who had already no-balled someone, was one of the umpires, but that is possibly being too cynical (the other umpire was Syd Buller who would play a very significant part in the tour as far as Griffin was concerned), and it was Jim Pothecary of Western Province who opened the attack with Neil Adcock. He did well, in fact, taking 4-55 in the first innings and dismissing Ron Headley, the son of George Headley, 'the Black Bradman', for a pair of spectacles, the phrase for 0 in both innings. Worcestershire struggled to save the follow-on, but Dick Richardson scored 72 before being bowled by Adcock and eventually, with some strong hitting by Len Coldwell at the end, Worcestershire saved the indignity of being required to follow on, and reached 235.

On the subject of Ron Headley, and without wishing to belabour a point, one would have liked to have asked the South Africans how it came about that a black man was able to take the field against them in England without the world coming to an end? One would like to think that some of the more intelligent or enlightened of the squad, or some of the younger idealists among them, would have liked to have asked a question about this. Why could this not happen in their own country?

Ignoring the counter attractions on TV on the Friday morning, McGlew and Goddard set about restoring their damaged reputations from their first innings, scoring quickly to allow the South Africans to declare at 144/1 and to set the home side 275 to win in about four hours. This was clearly beyond Worcestershire, but they might have held out for a draw. Instead, they collapsed pitifully for 141 and lost by 133 runs.

The manner of Worcestershire's defeat was surprising. It was not Adcock who caused the damage. Hugh Tayfield took two wickets but it was the slow left-armer Atholl McKinnon who took 7-42, spinning them out, mainly to catches on the off side.

Wisden says he was bowling round the wicket whereas Charles Fortune in *Cricket Overthrown* said that it was 'from over the wicket'. Not that it mattered. It was a fine bowling performance and the team now went on the short coach journey to Derby in a considerable state of confidence for the rest of the tour. McKinnon had clearly put down a marker for Test selection – the manager might have done better to pay attention – and the tour was off to a good start.

Anyone who bought the *Daily Mirror* on Saturday, 7 May to find out how the South Africans had done would have had to work hard to find mention of it beneath reams of material on the royal wedding and about that day's English FA Cup Final. But there was a report there on the second-last page written by Brian Chapman, extolling the virtues of Atholl McKinnon, albeit qualifying his praise by saying that he was no Hedley Verity, but mainly excoriating the Worcestershire batsmen who dished up 'lollipop catches' in an 'appalling exhibition of alleged batting'.

The next game against Derbyshire did not have any royal wedding as competition on the Saturday, but it did have the cup final, which was also on TV. This year it was Wolverhampton Wanderers v Blackburn Rovers and it was generally regarded as one of the poorer FA Cup Finals as Wolves won 3-0 but needed the help of an own goal and Blackburn having a man carried off to do so. Wolves might have won the league as well this year as they had done for the past two years in 1958 and 1959, but had lost out narrowly to Burnley a few days earlier.

The weather at Derby was splendid and the transistor radios of those listening to the football were a minor menace, but what no one could dispute was the excellence of the South African attack. This time Griffin did play, opening the bowling with Adcock, as Pothecary was first change. Not a no-ball was called by umpires Paul Gibb and Ron Aspinall, and the three pacemen ripped Derbyshire out for a mere 108 fairly soon after lunch. There was no excuse for Derbyshire about the pitch, and only three men reached double figures. The English press were all impressed by the pace attack and the consensus of opinion at this stage of the tour was that Griffin's action, although unusual and ungainly, was not illegal.

The gentlemen of the press were equally impressed by the batting as South Africa finished the day in total command of the game at 187/3 with McGlew and Pithey in their nineties. But those who thought and hoped that the throwing controversy might now be strangled at birth were confounded when Derbyshire's Harold Rhodes was called by umpire Paul Gibb six times in all for throwing. The weather was a great deal less pleasant on Monday, 9 May but McGlew was able to declare at 343/8, although neither he, Pithey nor O'Linn achieved a century (McLean was rested after his heroics at Worcester).

Derbyshire put up more of a fight this time but were still bowled out for 211 and lost by an innings, having no real answer to Neil Adcock who took 6-44 in a sustained display of fast aggressive bowling. Griffin was indeed no-balled near the end by Paul Gibb but it was for 'drag' at the bowler's end, and South Africa finished this game looking a very good side indeed, radiating confidence and a collective self-belief. Although the tour was still young, two good comfortable wins out of two (admittedly not against the strongest of English counties) meant things were looking very encouraging.

The weather, which had been good and tolerably warm (uncharacteristically good for the time of year, perhaps) up to now, then turned awkward when the Springboks went to Oxford. Only a few hours' play on the first day were possible with Oxford University reaching 77/4 before bad weather closed things down and did not relent. This gave the tourists the chance to see the city of the dreaming spires, and also allowed them rather neatly to avoid some scheduled anti-apartheid demonstrations which still went ahead in the rain while the cricketers were sitting comfortably in the cinema!

Serious business resumed on Saturday, 14 May when the South Africans went to take on Essex at Ilford. Essex, chronic underperformers in the County Championship, although not without their occasional moments of glory, were, on the face of it, stronger opposition than either Worcestershire or Derbyshire. They had two England stalwarts in Trevor Bailey and Doug Insole, although it would have to be said that the best of the Test match days of these two were behind them. There were also a few rising stars like young all-rounder Barry Knight, and Joseph Milner, himself a South African, with perhaps a point to prove to his fellow countrymen.

The game attracted a good crowd, and although everyone focussed on the umpires Charlie Elliott and John Langridge, the game passed without any no-ball incidents. Indeed, it was yet another good game for the tourists, who on the Saturday shot Essex out for 98 on a green-top pitch after recent rain. Neither opening batsman troubled the scorers, as Adcock and Griffin seemed to be running riot. Insole was out for 4, Bailey for 2 and the only real resistance came from Milner who put on 29 before Tayfield had him caught. It was another very encouraging performance by the Springboks who deployed five bowlers, all of whom returned good figures, Tayfield in particular, taking 5-43.

McGlew himself was rested with a slight injury, so Trevor Goddard was in charge. Jonathan Fellows-Smith had not taken a great part on the tour so far, but at Ilford he announced to the English public that he was back with a fine innings of 109 not out, attracting the admiration of *Wisden* for being 'sound in defence but quick to punish the loose ball especially with the drive', as the South Africans reached 287. Enjoying the somewhat eccentric nickname of 'Pom Pom', Fellows-Smith had been in England before, played a few games for Oxford University and Northants in the past, but without distinguishing himself.

But the star was the veteran Trevor Bailey whose controlled medium-pacers were never likely to bamboozle the batsmen even on a tricky pitch like this one. But Bailey obeyed the basic principles of line and length and returned excellent figures of 40-5-81-7 and perhaps caused a few to wonder whether his Test days were really behind him.

Never the most exciting of batsmen, it has to be said, and often worthy of the nickname 'barnacle' because of his ability to stick around, Trevor had a thorough knowledge of the game and in later years became one of the leading commentators on *Test Match Special*, giving birth to phrases like 'more than somewhat' to describe an excellent innings or spell of bowling.

Trevor was also very much a 'keep politics out of sport' sympathiser. Many years later when he was on *Test Match Special*, and when an interview had been arranged with Peter Hain of the 'Stop the Seventies Tour' movement from 1970, Trevor declined the opportunity to talk to him and even asked for his shifts to be rearranged so that he would not be on commentary immediately before or after lunch interval, so that he would not have to meet Mr Hain!

But in this match it was the other Essex veteran, Doug Insole who organised the resistance in the second innings, and his duel with Tayfield was a sight to behold and won hands down by Insole, who hit 105 before eventually falling lbw to him. These two, of course, had 'form', having met in the past and it was rumoured that they did not like each other on a personal level either.

Tayfield's figures of 1-118 were less than flattering, and once again it was Adcock who did the damage, although acting captain Goddard came on at the end and took 3-10 to mop up the tail.

Essex's total of 274 was enough to avoid an innings defeat, but it meant that the South Africans needed only 86 to win. The pitch was now badly damaged and the South Africans made a bad start, losing Goddard, Duckworth, O'Linn and McLean cheaply before the less experienced young men Carlstein and Wesley steadied the ship and saw South Africa home by six wickets.

By now most players had had a 'turn' at either batting or bowling and had proved themselves capable of some things in English conditions, but the weather stayed miserable when the South Africans visited Fenners to play Cambridge. In spite of the unpropitious conditions, the tourists had another fine win over the students. This victory was all the more creditable because they were behind on the first innings and a potential embarrassing defeat was imminent.

The students had some fine players like Roger Prideaux who played for Northants in future years, but the man who did the damage to the South Africans was another South African called James Brodie who took 5-47 as the tourists were dismissed for 145, some 47 runs behind the Cambridge University total. But once again the ferocious Adcock excelled himself taking 6-26 as the students were skittled for 80, leaving the South Africans to score only 128 to win. They achieved this for the loss of three wickets as captain McGlew led the way with 54 not out.

This game was played in cold miserable conditions throughout and had to take second place in public attention to what is generally regarded as being one of the best football matches of all time. It took place at Hampden Park, Glasgow, and was the fifth final of the new and revolutionary European Cup tournament. It was between Real Madrid and Eintracht Frankfurt and was shown throughout the world on TV. Real Madrid won 7-3 with Puskás, Gento and di Stéfano all at their best. It was played on the evening of Wednesday, 18 May, after the first day's play at Fenners. The South Africans, not all of them necessarily football fans (although some were, like Sid O'Linn who had played professional football for Charlton Athletic) sat in front of a television and enjoyed it.

But things now began to heat up for the South Africans, although not yet in the meteorological sense. The next game, against the MCC at Lord's, was generally regarded as a trial for the Test match with some ambitious young Englishmen given a chance to put goods in the shop window, as it were, for Test selection. The MCC team was captained by Colin Cowdrey and contained men like Ted Dexter and Mike Smith. South Africa's team, as it turned out, was more or less the team that would take the field in the first Test match, except for the important omission of Adcock. His position was assured. There was no point in exposing him here.

The very term MCC needs explanation. It stands for Marylebone Cricket Club, and in the public perception of the time it tended to mean 'England' in the cricketing sense. In the same way that games were played between 'the South Africans' and English counties, but Test matches were England v South Africa, so too abroad on winter tours the MCC would play against Natal or Queensland, whereas Test matches would see England play Australia or South Africa. There were several layers of history, tradition and sheer snobbery here, and now and again the TV or radio commentators would, in a cricketing Freudian slip, talk about 'England' when they meant MCC and vice versa. Only the otiose, the pedantic and the ultra class-conscious would object or even notice.

The game was to be on BBC television with commentary from men like Brian Johnston and Peter West. Television was important in that it brought cricket within the reach and grasp of so many people. The cameras were only at one end, and the coverage lacked the sophistication of play-backs and action replays. 'Snicko', reviews and ball tracking were not even dreamt about, and the coverage of the game depended to a very large extent on which other sports would be on the Saturday *Grandstand* programme, and although there was a two-hour slot in the morning for nothing other than cricket, the start was delayed by rain! Nevertheless, for all its limitations, cricket fans who found it impossible, for reasons of distance, to travel to grounds like Lord's, have a very strong affection for BBC cricket in the early days of television. We could actually see what men like Jackie McGlew and Colin Cowdrey looked like!

We also learned things like, for example, Brian Johnston enjoyed 'Yorkshire pud' for lunch. Peter West was a brilliant commentator with his very English middle-class accent and mannerisms, but, although he commentated on other sports like rugby and compered *Come Dancing*, he always said that cricket was his first love, so much so that he was editor of the *Playfair Cricket Annual* for several years.

The game itself, played in poor conditions on all three days, was a disappointment. Described by several commentators as being played in 'two-sweater' weather conditions, there were very few outstanding individual performances. The miserable weather affected the South Africans more than it did the Englishmen who are, after all, used to such weather!

The highest score on either side was Trevor Goddard's 56, the bowling was poor as well and even though Colin Cowdrey claimed the extra half-hour to try and force a win, the MCC were never really close and the South Africans finished with three wickets in hand. The game did not give either side an advantage in the imminent Test match series, although South Africa were confirmed in what they already knew, the fact that they needed Neil Adcock. Cowdrey captained the side well enough for the MCC (or England, if you prefer!) to appoint him as captain for the first three of the five Test matches – a curious decision in a way. Cowdrey would have felt better – and so would the players, one feels – if he had been appointed for the whole series. Cowdrey had taken over the captaincy from his friend Peter May halfway through the tour of the West Indies after May had been taken ill and been forced to return home. In the event, Cowdrey was captain for the whole five Test matches.

And yet, for all the disappointment of the actual cricket, this was the game which would more or less define the tour. It ensured that cricket would become and remain the main topic of conversation for a large part of the summer – and sadly, for the wrong reasons.

All the drama came on the first day, and it concerned Geoff Griffin. It was the first time that most of the spectators and those watching on television had seen him. Fair-haired, nice-looking, the sort of boy that middle-aged, middle-class matrons would all like to put their arms around – not necessarily for basic reproductive purposes (younger ladies might have permitted themselves a few hankerings!) but because he looked as if, in this strange and faraway country, he could do with a little looking-after and molly-coddling, particularly when it was cold and wet and when the umpires were being cruel to him. Griffin conducted himself like a gentleman throughout.

The umpires were Frank Lee and John Langridge. Lee had never seen him before, but Langridge had been with him at Essex the previous week and seen nothing untoward in his action. McGlew won the toss and inserted the MCC. Griffin opened from the Nursery End and Pothecary from the Pavilion End. Other than a dropped catch by Tayfield off Griffin, which would have got rid of Cowdrey, it was a sedate start on one of the coldest days that Lord's had seen for some time.

Griffin had bowled four overs, the general opinion in the crowd and the media being that although Griffin's action was unusual in that he was a bit double-jointed and that he was very front-on, it was not necessarily illegal, and he did not seem to be gaining any unfair advantage by his delivery. Frank Lee at square leg did and said nothing, although ironically Griffin had been no-balled by bowler's-end umpire John Langridge for 'drag', which meant in 1960 having his back foot over the bowling crease line as the ball was delivered.

Charles Fortune makes a salient point. He tells us that weeks earlier before a game had been played or a ball bowled in anger, he had watched Griffin from several angles when the tourists were practising. From where an umpire placed himself for a right-handed batsman when the bowling was from the Nursery End, i.e. where the umpire was looking slightly downhill at Griffin, there seemed to be little wrong with his action, but when he watched him from the Tavern side of the ground, it was a different matter.

Cowdrey took a single, and left-handed John Edrich now faced the bowling. Lee moved to square leg for the left-hander, giving him a new perspective and then created history by calling Griffin for a no-ball, making him the first overseas player to be called for throwing at Lord's, it was believed. Amidst a cemetery silence (for the crowd was actually quite shocked), McGlew took Griffin off. He was then brought back some time later at the other end so that Lee could not call him.

His first ball in that spell may well have been significant in that he bowled Ted Dexter. Charles Fortune described it thus: 'Dexter stood fast-footed with his bat aloft as the ball came towards him. He still stood for some seconds and obviously unbelieving, to gaze at the broken wicket before accepting the evidence of his own eyes. He had been bowled making no stroke by a sharp break-back. Dexter his head aloft and his bat swinging as if there were anger in the man, stalked away.'

What this fine piece of writing seems to indicate is that the ball had come on him too soon, something that often happens when the ball has been thrown with a bent arm rather than bowled with a straight one. Perhaps that is why there was 'anger in the man'. It is hard, however, not to believe that the Dexter reaction at this critical stage of the game and of the tour played a large part in what happened in other games. Had Dexter merely headed for the pavilion, as McGlew notably did when he was given out on a later controversial occasion, things might have been different.

But here was Ted Dexter, arguably England's best player, from the champagne and caviar county of Sussex and a man whom the establishment would have identified with, making it plain, without incurring any charge of dissent or disputing the umpire's decision, that he thought he had been cheated out by a throw. To believe that there was no 'politics' in Dexter's actions seems to be very naïve indeed. Dexter himself may have been making a point about 'chuckers' for he was very conscious that he had not had a good tour in Australia against the alleged 'chuckers' there.

And this 'Dexter' ball may have affected Langridge, who now called Griffin several times, on one occasion for the same ball that Lee also called him for drag – a rare if not unprecedented occurrence. The South Africans now had the reasonable point that if Langridge called him at Lord's, why had he not done so at Ilford? The answer of course would have been that he was calling him, or not, on the basis of each individual ball. Indeed, Langridge and Lee were both quoted as saying that Griffin's action was 'basically fair' apart from the occasional ball.

This did not convince the South Africans. It looked as if Langridge had called Griffin to show solidarity with Lee. They had clearly discussed the matter (as umpires do). Perhaps he was under pressure from the MCC, perhaps he did not want to be considered to be 'soft' on bowling actions, but then a further strange thing occurred when, in the second innings, Griffin was allowed to bowl unmolested as this dull and rather uninteresting game of cricket continued. It was as if the point had been made on the Saturday, and then the matter was put to bed.

The point was certainly made, and a leading story had been found for both the broadsheets and the tabloid newspapers. Very soon everyone, particularly those who had never seen him bowl, had a strong opinion about his action and to a very large extent it depended on which newspaper one read. The 'sensational' press as they were called (they were not as yet all tabloids) used phrases like 'chuck out the chuckers' and even hinted that some of the other South African bowlers were suspect as well, while the more restrained *Times*, *Telegraph* and *Manchester Guardian* were of the opinion that some remedial action should be taken or that the issue should be investigated more thoroughly. Godfrey Evans writing in *The People* advised the South Africans to send for Peter Heine now, for he was convinced that Griffin was a chucker.

Such film as exists now is unsatisfactory and inconclusive, but the one man that emerged with total credit was Griffin himself, who said nothing. He was of course bound by his contract to do so, but he resisted any monetary temptation to give any quotes, even obliquely through someone else. Indeed, it is something that must be said about the South African party as a whole. No matter what happened on the tour – and it pretty well went downhill in every respect from that point on – dignity was the watchword.

One is tempted to use phrases like 'they did their country proud'. In fact, they transcended that. Their country really had little to be proud of after Sharpeville and their absurd statements about black people being a lot happier under apartheid than any other form of government, but these 15 cricketers were icons of good behaviour, always well dressed, polite and courteous with an absence of bad behaviour on and off the field. What happened and was said behind closed doors will never be known, but the image projected was a positive one, and gradually as the tour went on, sympathy grew for them. Even when in later years it appeared that some of them got themselves involved in pro-apartheid politics, they were remembered by those who met them in 1960 as great ambassadors for the sport. As for me, they became my heroes.

The few days after the MCC game saw several meetings. On Wednesday, 25 May, the MCC issued a statement: 'Representatives of MCC and Mr AD Nourse met the umpires at Lord's after the match, MCC v South Africa and discussed the no-balling of G Griffin in this game. The umpires stated that, in their opinion, Griffin's basic action was fair, and only on occasions were they not entirely satisfied with the absolute fairness of a delivery.' The statement was bland, tactful but really did not say very much that one could not have already guessed. Nor did it seem to point to any long-term solution to the problem. A couple of days later a further statement was issued, either clarifying or further obfuscating (depending on one's viewpoint) the first one.

This one stated: 'In the light of some of the interpretations of the statement issued to the press at the conclusion of the match MCC v South Africans, concerning the no-balling of G Griffin, the full MCC committee, meeting yesterday, decided that they must make it clear that this announcement did no more than state the individual views concerning this bowler of the two umpires standing in this match. The MCC are giving constant attention to the problem of unfair bowling; they are determined to eradicate such bowling and emphasise that they will give their full support to any action umpires may take to further this end.'

Once again it depended on your viewpoint, but this could be taken as meaning that 'chucking' was condoned – a point made by the Labour-orientated *Daily Herald* with bees in its bonnet about both racial segregation in South Africa and inherent snobbishness in the MCC – or you could take the opposite view that Charles Fortune the South African journalist did, that 'this was a clear directive to umpires to be after Geoff Griffin'. Yet another 'take' on that statement was that it didn't say anything at all.

It is of course obvious to any outsider that the umpires and specifically the umpire who stands at square leg ALONE can decide whether or not a man throws. It is basically what they are paid for. There was therefore a very strong argument in favour of leaving the umpires to decide. But that was what emphatically was NOT happening here. Self-interested and intrusive fingers of journalists and administrators were poked into all sorts of political pies.

Meanwhile, as Griffin himself lay low, an extraordinary cricket match was taking place at Northampton. The South Africans batted first and hit 461/3 declared in a magnificent display of batting. Trevor Goddard scored 186 not out and Roy McLean 180 as poor Frank Tyson, the hero of the 1954/55 England tour of Australia, was put to the sword and conceded 101 runs in 26 overs for only one wicket – a rather fortuitous 'hit wicket' against McLean. This seemed to have guaranteed South Africa against defeat, except for two things – the fightback in the Northants batting and a few wrong decisions by Jackie McGlew, for which he was rightly pilloried in the South African press, for it was the first defeat of the tour. Perhaps Jackie's mind was on other things.

Northampton, spearheaded by Raman Subba Row who scored 108, batted sensibly and reached 363 giving the South Africans a lead of 98 but still keeping Northants in the game. They were particularly severe on Tayfield, who took six wickets eventually but at the cost of 123 runs. Tayfield was over-bowled with 46.2 overs, one felt, but the other bowlers, with the exception of the ever reliable Adcock, failed to impress.

Still, with a lead of 98, all the tourists really needed was a reasonably quick 200 to put the game out of the reach of Northants. But McGlew played about with the batting order and, with the laudable intention of giving everyone match practice, opened with Pithey and Duckworth. The only success was the Rhodesian Duckworth who scored 51 not out as the rest subsided to a miserable 94/8 by the time McGlew himself came to the crease. He steered the total past 100 and then declared when he and Duckworth could have put on a few more. He dangled the target of exactly 200 in slightly less than three hours, a reasonable possibility.

McGlew possibly deserves credit for making a game of it when it could all have fizzled out into the tamest of draws, but he still wanted to win. Northants batted sensibly and well, reaching the total in the last over for the loss of six wickets. McGlew's bowlers once again let him down with Pothecary and Fellows-Smith (whose big opportunity this might have been) failing to rip through the Northants batsmen. Northants, therefore, by no means one of the more fashionable counties and who would finish in the middle of the table at the end of the season, became the first county to lower the colours of the tourists. It was a shame that it was a midweek game and overshadowed by other events affecting the tourists, but it was a moment of glory for the Northamptonshire club and their small band of spectators. Such moments were few and far between in the history of this underperforming club. For the Springboks, the lesson was clear. They needed Geoff Griffin. McGlew's generous declaration would also have a few implications and effects on his thinking later on in the summer.

The issue of 'sporting declarations' was a live one in the County Championship. Should a captain always guard against defeat, or should he give the opposition a chance by 'keeping them interested'? Spectators would of course want to see meaningful cricket on the last day, and the timing of a declaration was a very important thing. The really crucial thing, however, was how the captain's players reacted to the declaration, whether generous or otherwise. Clearly in this case, if the finger is to be pointed at McGlew, it must also be pointed at his players.

And so, Griffin was chosen for the next game, a short distance from Northampton at Trent Bridge, Nottingham where the third Test match would be played in July. It turned out to be another tragedy for Geoff Griffin, for here two other and lesser-known umpires, TJ Bartley and WH Copson, both no-balled him, eight times in all for throwing and seven times for dragging. It was clear that the young man had a problem, and what was noticeable was that the large crowd – the weather was good – showed little reaction when Griffin was called, neither cheering nor booing. It was not clear whether the sporadic applause was directed in sympathy to Griffin, or to show appreciation for the bravery of the umpires.

It was also clear from reading reports by respected writers like John Arlott and Charles Fortune that, in their view, there was no clear distinction between the balls that were called and the balls that were not. It was as if the umpires were calling only a token few to indicate their disapproval of his action. During the game, it was announced that Griffin would now go to Alf Gover's school in London, commonly known as 'the cricket doctor' to see if anything could be done to solve the problem there. It seemed like a drowning man clutching at straws.

In passing one can surely give the umpires a certain amount of sympathy as well. I have been an umpire and can confirm that no umpire likes calling a bowler for a no-ball for throwing – although there was one later in the 1960 summer who seemed to carry his duties to over-zealous and unnecessary extremes – for it is such a draconian step. There is far more at stake here than the one run given for the penalty, for it has such a huge effect on the bowler's career. It would be hard to believe that either Tom Bartley or Bill Copson, both very experienced umpires who had played the game with distinction as well, took this step lightly, or slept soundly in their beds before and after doing so.

My own umpiring experiences, if I may expand on this, came in the 1980s and 1990s in the recreational Scottish League where players were generally amateurs, although one professional per side was allowed. No one's livelihood was really at stake, and on the Monday, I would return to my day job of teaching in a secondary school while the players returned to their offices, factories and schools.

Inevitably, however, there were a few bowlers whose actions were suspect. I was never looked upon as a 'cowardly' umpire, nor, I think, an over-aggressive one. Other decisions like lbw, caught behind, run out and the fitness or otherwise of conditions for play seldom bothered me, and I usually shrugged my shoulders at the thought that there were several players who felt victimised by a wrong decision or two on my part. Such things happen, I reckoned. You can never please everybody!

But with bowling actions, I was never so phlegmatic. I was always aware that umpire A had called him and umpire B hadn't in previous games, and that everyone seemed to be looking to me at square leg to decide. I felt lonely and vulnerable. I was always willing to hide behind any official directive that 'his action had been cleared' by someone or other, and I remember an odd feeling of relief and delight when a colleague phoned the ground to say that his car had broken down and that he wouldn't be able to attend. With astonishing haste and enthusiasm I told the captains that I would do 'bowler's end' all the time, and a member of the batting side would have to do 'square leg' and that I would 'rely on his honesty'. This way, I could avoid a difficult decision about a nice young man who seemed to have a strange action! Coward!

I recall only once calling a fellow for 'chucking'. He didn't do it every ball, but just occasionally when striving for extra pace, he opened his chest and bent his arm. I let it go the first time, but then called him the second time. The silence was deafening as everyone turned and looked at me. I didn't have to do it again … but it was not a happy memory, all the more so because the bowler was of an Asian background and I feared allegations of racism! It didn't happen but I lost a night's sleep fearing that something might!

On another occasion with another club, I (irregularly and improperly) told a captain that I did not like the action of one of his spinners, and that it might be an idea to bowl him from my end. A word to the wise is often enough, and my square leg colleague saw nothing out of order (nor did the batting side) as the spinner mopped up the tail of the innings. I shouldn't have done this, but it saved a great deal of bother, and to this day no one (other than the captain) knew anything about it. Maybe the bowler was legal after all!

Such are the agonies of umpiring but, apart from that, there was a great deal of interesting cricket played by both sides in the Nottinghamshire game. Trevor Goddard had opened the bowling with Griffin and took five wickets as Notts batted carefully and sensibly to reach the acceptable score of 280 at the end of the Saturday. Veteran Reggie Simpson top-scored with 66 after openers Hill and Winfield put on 99 for the first wicket. Without Adcock and with Griffin having his problems, there was no real bite in the Springboks with Fellows-Smith, McKinnon and Tayfield all failing to trouble the batsmen to any great extent.

Monday saw five South African batsmen pass 50 but none of them achieving the three figures as they reached 433, McGlew's 68 being especially creditable as he was suffering from backache which caused him to leave the field for treatment for a spell. There did not seem to be many problems in the South African batting as the first Test now appeared on the horizon, but once again questions were raised about the efficacy of their bowling as Notts put on 193/4 to save the game without any real problem.

And so ended the month of May. It had been an eventful month for the South Africans. The plus points had been the good form in the games against the counties (even the game that they had lost had been brought about by a few miscalculations by Jackie McGlew for which he actually earned a few plaudits in the English press for his contribution to 'brighter cricket') and in addition quite a few batsmen – McLean, Goddard, Fellows-Smith and McGlew himself – had had good scores. Against that, there was the major problem about Griffin. He was a fine strike bowler, but clearly he was likely to be no-balled out of the tour and possibly the game altogether unless Alf Gover managed to find a solution to the problem. But time was running out with the first Test match starting on 9 June.

Politically, things had not been quite as bad as had been expected. There had been demonstrations and letters to newspapers, but as yet the cricket had not been disrupted. It was always a potential problem, however, and one often wonders whether the sting might not have been taken out of things by the team together issuing a statement dissociating themselves from apartheid, deploring Sharpeville, making a few vague statements about wanting to work for racial integration in cricket in South Africa and looking forward to the day when they would be able to organise a tour to the West Indies or have India or Pakistan visiting South Africa.

Sadly, no one ever really thought of this, and the reason seems to be that so many of the players themselves were supporters of the apartheid system in which they had been brought up and which had done well for them. Waite's book *Perchance to Bowl* makes his position clear, and one or two of them, even McGlew himself, subsequently involved themselves in pro-apartheid politics, standing at one point for the National Party. Yet it is so hard to believe that so many charming, intelligent young men could be so collectively misguided.

Another thing that they might have considered doing was sending for a replacement for Griffin in case things turned out badly for him, as indeed they did. *The People* newspaper had already suggested sending for Peter Heine. He could have been flown up fairly soon, even perhaps in time for the first Test match. In addition, there was an absolute host of young South African fast bowlers playing for one or other of the English counties, like Joseph Milner of Essex or even James Brodie, whom they had already been on the wrong side of when they played Cambridge University. They might have been good enough as an insurance policy, particularly as the obvious replacement for Griffin within the party, Jim Pothecary was not as yet producing the goods.

But no effort was made at this point to send for anyone else. The South Africans would have cause to regret that.

*The South Africans
arrive in early April*

Harold Macmillan, Prime Minister of Great Britain who warned everyone of what was to happen in his famous Wind of Change speech

Rev David Sheppard, England Test cricketer and a well-known anti-apartheid campaigner. He declined to have anything to do with the tour

The aftermath of Sharpeville in March 1960

An anti-apartheid protest in South Africa

Jackie McGlew puts his team through catching practice at Lord's in April

Jackie McGlew and Trevor Goddard open the Tour against the Duke of Norfolk's XI

The 1960 South Africans at Worcester for the start of the tour.
Back Row: J Pothecary, HJ Tayfield, G Griffin, AH McKinnon, P Carlstein, JP Fellows-Smith, NAT Adcock, CAR Duckworth, A Pithey, C Wesley, S O'Linn, M McLennan (Scorer)
Front Row: RA McLean, DJ McGlew, Dudley Nourse (Manager), TL Goddard, JHB Waite

John Waite, South Africa's wicketkeeper/batsman

Neil Adcock, fast bowler

Geoff Griffin

Some indication of Griffin's bent arm as he bowls?

Peter Walker is bowled by Griffin at Lord's. It is the second ball of Griffin's hat-trick

Griffin, having been no-balled four times in one over, has to bowl underarm to complete this over in the Exhibition Match

Jonathan Fellows Smith batting at Valentine's Park, Ilford against Essex

Brian Statham, England's reliable fast bowler in 1960

Colin Cowdrey, England's captain

John Arlott, cricket commentator, writer and journalist with strong anti-apartheid views

Brian Johnston, cricket commentator

CHAPTER FIVE

EDGBASTON

THE FIRST Test match of a series sets the tone. Often there is a bit of spar-boxing going on, with both sides sizing each other up, and a draw often occurs. On the other hand, a victory for either side puts them in a strong position, as the press tend to focus on the problems of the defeated, and it is not long before words like 'beleaguered' and 'demoralised' begin to make their appearance as the defeated captain, whose future is inevitably 'in jeopardy', 'desperately tries to rally his troops'. It is therefore vital not to lose the first Test match in any series.

It may be that the first few days of June lulled South Africa into a false sense of security. There were two victories, both achieved in two days, and an optimistic report back from Alf Gover about Geoff Griffin, who had been working hard at Alf's school to sort out the no-ball problems. Gover himself would have sympathised with Griffin. He had been a great fast bowler for Surrey in the 1930s, and although he had never really broken through to any great extent at Test level, he had taken over 200 wickets in one season (1937). He had had problems in overstepping the crease and being no-balled, but never for throwing. It was as a coach that he became famous. As early as 1960, he had built up a mighty reputation.

The Minor Counties had hard luck against the South Africans at Stoke. A man retired hurt in each innings, and the man who was injured in the first innings was unable to bat in the second, but in any case, the Minor Counties men had no real answer to Neil Adcock, whose figures of 5-37 and 5-31 spoke for themselves. The batting contained a century from McGlew and a good knock of 90 from Colin Wesley, the diminutive young Natal left-hander (his nickname was 'Titch') who thus announced himself on the scene and staked a claim for a Test-match place.

One could sympathise with the brave, enthusiastic, recreational cricketers from the Minor Counties, some of whom were clearly overwhelmed by the occasion. Less compassion is possible for Glamorgan, the tourists' next opponents. *Wisden* states uncompromisingly that: 'There was no excuse for two feeble batting displays by Glamorgan,' and it was all the more disappointing considering that there was a crowd of 10,000 at the Cardiff Arms Park, some of whom consoled themselves with drunken but good-natured renderings of 'Land of My Fathers' once they had visited a beer tent or two for an anaesthetic to dull the effects of what was happening on the field. Their rugby team usually put up better performances than this.

Glamorgan, who had only been a county in the County Championship since 1921, were looked upon as the representatives of Wales. They had had their moments and fine players like Johnnie Clay, by this point retired, and Wilfred Wooller who was still playing. In 1960, with all the flags flying and a team containing two men called Evans, one called Rees, another called Jones, they were characteristically Welsh. More pertinently, there was also the tall Peter Walker who had just been selected for the first Test match at Edgbaston and it was the chance to show the value of Welsh cricket, something that had often been jeered at in the past. Sadly, they could not raise their game and *Wisden's* assessment of 'feeble batting displays' was spot on.

The South Africans had a major boost with the return of Griffin. Alf Gover was confident that Griffin would now pass scrutiny in the eyes of the umpires and that he 'had endeavoured to stop the wrist waggle [sic] just before Griffin's final action' and that he (Gover) had tried to make him (Griffin) bowl more with a side-on action rather than front-on. He had had five sessions of intensive work at the Spencer Cricket Club in Wandsworth, and Gover was now sure that the problem had gone. Gover put his reputation on the line by this bold and (as it turned out) somewhat unwise and premature statement. It was a shame because Gover, himself a formidable fast bowler for Surrey in the past, had done so much to produce and develop good cricketers and would indeed continue to do so until he retired at an advanced age in 1989.

Griffin was chosen to play at Cardiff but bowled only six innocuous overs in the first innings as Trevor Goddard and Jonathan Fellows-Smith with accurate 'military medium' pace shot the Welshmen out for a pathetic 87 to the almost tangible disappointment of the Cardiff crowd. The South Africans then simply took over, with McGlew and Goddard putting on 256 for the first wicket and batting Glamorgan out of the game. When Glamorgan went in again, in comparative terms they put up a little more resistance than they had first time round, but were still dismissed for 138 with only Gilbert Parkhouse able to hold up his head with a reasonable show of aggression in his 67. But Glamorgan fell to the spin bowling of McKinnon and Tayfield, and the game finished before stumps on the Monday night, leaving the South Africans with two days to prepare for the Edgbaston Test match. In retrospect, it might have been better for the Springboks if they had faced more demanding opposition, and had had to deploy Griffin for longer.

Pothecary, Wesley, Duckworth and McKinnon were the unlucky South Africans who had to sit out the first Test match, and O'Linn, Fellows-Smith and Griffin were given their Test debuts. The attack consisted of two fast men, Griffin and Adcock, Goddard and Fellows-Smith were the change bowlers and Tayfield was the spinner. The batting looked solid enough with McGlew and Goddard opening, followed by Pithey, McLean, Waite, Carlstein and O'Linn. That seemed, prima facie, good enough to deal with anything that even Statham and Trueman could throw (or in the context of 1960 we had better say 'bowl'!) at them.

But the South African bowling looked a bit short. Adcock was good, but Griffin needed to be sure of not no-balling, and was clearly under the pressure of intense media scrutiny. The medium pacers, in spite of some good performances against the counties, were unproven at Test match level, and veteran spinner Hugh Tayfield had already shown himself to be vulnerable on this tour. He was, however, an unpredictable sort of character, and one never really knew what to expect from him.

England's team was Colin Cowdrey as captain, Geoff Pullar to open with him, then a very strong middle order of Ted Dexter, Raman Subba Row and Mike Smith. Wicketkeeper was Jim Parks, then came newcomers Peter

Walker and Bob Barber, with spinner Ray Illingworth and the two fast strike bowlers in Brian Statham and Fred Trueman. The two fast men were at their peak, and they complemented each other – one from Lancashire and one from Yorkshire. Trueman revelled in his nickname of 'Fiery Fred' and was an irascible character, very popular in spite of his occasionally boorish behaviour. Any young fan who approached him never knew whether he would get his autograph or a volley of abuse. Sometimes Fred would ruffle the youngster's hair, ask him where he came from, and did he play the game, etc. Other times he would ignore his fans or even be rude to them. Being the brilliant bowler that he was, he often got away with it. In later years he would feature in *Test Match Special*, opinionated and dogmatic with his catchphrase being 'I don't understand what's going on out there' if he disapproved of a bowling change, for example. He was well summed up in one of his obituaries as 'an admirable bowler but not always a loveable man'.

Brian Statham, on the other hand, commonly known as 'George' for some reason (possibly because Lancashire, who had always had loads of men called George, suddenly one day found themselves without one, and they chose Statham to be 'George'), had a curious slinging sort of action, but was totally reliable with accuracy and pace. He and Trueman worked as a pair, getting wickets for one another, unsettling the opposition so that the batsman heaved a sigh of relief as he got to the other end, while the other bowler then took advantage of the batsman's false sense of security. Trueman tended to rely on away swing, encouraging a waft by an irresponsible batsman; Statham went for the stumps. On their day, they could be virtually unbeatable.

On the morning of the Test match, the *Birmingham Daily Post* reported that groundsman Bernard Flack thought that he had prepared a perfect wicket for a Test match, and that everything was in order for a good game, and that the weather forecast was good. Security precautions were tight and arrangements had been made to ensure that the wicket would be well protected overnight, because no one excluded the possibility of anti-apartheid protests. Out of a total membership of 12,000, only four members, however, had written to say that they would not be attending the game for 'conscience reasons'.

Nevertheless, advance bookings were disappointing, and this was a source of concern for the Warwickshire club, because in a country which normally played only five Tests per summer and had six Test match grounds in Edgbaston, Trent Bridge, Old Trafford, Headingley, Lord's and The Oval, a Test match could not be guaranteed.

June 1960 was my final few weeks of primary education. The following term I was to go to the 'big' school, the local academy, something that filled me with apprehension but also a certain feeling of excitement. My primary school was little more than five minutes from my house, so when lunch time came at 12.45pm I could charge home and be ensconced in front of the TV well before 1pm so that I had a clean half-hour's cricket watching before lunch at 1.30pm. And the great advantage was that everyone was out, I had the house to myself ... and nobody spoke!

Peter West and Brian Johnston told us that they were off to enjoy their beef roast followed by cucumber or anchovy sandwiches. I, on the other hand had to be content with cheese sandwiches and tomato soup which my mother, now working as a dinner lady at the school, left for me. She shook her head at my new-found obsession with cricket but tolerated it.

School meant that I could not see any of the afternoon play (other than on the Saturday) and when the evening session was going on, the BBC did not oblige other than for a few minutes at the end, from 6.15pm, when they showed you the closing overs and gave a summary of the day. And then, of course, there were the following morning's newspapers to bring me up to date. It was an obsessive, almost autistic existence. The rest of the world did not really seem to matter when there was a Test match on. My friends looked at me almost pityingly but they knew that I would be back when the game was over. Football was their obsession, with cricket a passing interest, and indeed a game of cricket with a tennis ball and cheap bat out of Woolworths was not unknown. With me, it was the other way round! Cricket was the thing, although football sufficed when there was no cricket.

The first day's play at Edgbaston was disappointing, with England reaching 175/3. It was not the kind of day that would bring the crowds back in huge numbers. There were several stoppages for showers and that seemed to disrupt both the batting and the bowling, and generally speaking, the feeling was one of anticlimax, with Brian Chapman of the *Daily Mirror* of the opinion that the 'boycott brigade' (those who stayed away to protest against apartheid) were the lucky ones. The attendance was less than 10,000, about half the number that had attended the Roses match between Yorkshire and Lancashire a few days previously. Not all of the absentees were because of conscience reasons, however, one felt. The uncertain weather and the fact that Thursday was a working day all played their part.

Colin Cowdrey won the toss and batted. He himself perished for 3, having nibbled at an Adcock flyer, Ted Dexter showed some stroke play for his 52 before missing completely a ball from Tayfield and being bowled, and Geoff Pullar, having scored a patient and possibly ponderous 37, was out to a diving catch by McLean off Goddard. At the end, Mike Smith and Raman Subba Row were still in, but the batting performance could most charitably be described as 'solid' rather than anything else. It was not one of 'brighter cricket's' better days.

For their part, the South Africans would have been disappointed with their bowling performance. The weather was blustery, but Adcock was uncharacteristically wayward, and occasionally short of a length trying too hard to dig the ball in on a surface which did not really give him too much lift, the ball that accounted for Cowdrey being an exception to the rule. Wicketkeeper John Waite in *Perchance to Bowl*, his whimsical and occasionally irreverent account of this game, states that, 'For the first few overs of the day, I began to believe that I was keeping goal for Eintracht in their European Cup Final against Real Madrid at Glasgow,' (Real Madrid had won 7-3) so erratic and unpredictable were the first few overs! That remark might not have gone down too well with some of his bowlers, one feels!

But the big 'victory' for the Springboks was that Griffin's new, reformed bowling action passed its test with both umpires, one of them being John Langridge who had called him before. Eddie Phillipson similarly had no objection, and in that sense the young South African had a good day. Waite denies categorically that there was any plot on the part of the South Africans to get a fielder to stand at square leg and block the view of the square leg umpire! But the passing of the examination came at a price. Clearly nervous and unhappy, the fair-haired youngster seemed to have lost a little pace and certainly lost accuracy. He was working hard at his action, and although there were still some in the press and the public who thought that he threw, the general consensus was that the problem may well have been solved with this new side-on action, which he had developed and practised at Gover's school. His figures at the end of the innings, however, were 1-61 from 21 overs, and that cannot have given either himself or his team-mates any satisfaction at all.

England possibly had the better of that first day, but a blow came when it was announced that Geoff Pullar had broken a bone in his wrist and was effectively out of the rest of the game (he would in fact bat at no. 11 with one hand in the second innings) and indeed for a few games to come. The Lancastrian was a likeable character with the nickname of 'Noddy', which may have had something to do with the Enid Blyton character, but Brian Johnston told us it was more to do with his habit of 'nodding off' in the dressing room after he had been dismissed, and even during boring team talks.

Close of play was 175/3, and it was summed up by John Waite who said, 'Had Maurice Chevalier been among the spectators, he would have had little for which to thank heaven except the beautiful girls who tried their utmost to concentrate upon the cricket up in the members' stand.

'Even "Lord Edward's" (Ted Dexter) lovely young wife had smothered many a yawn.'

The innings plodded on the next day, most of the bowling being done by Tayfield and Goddard with Griffin used sparingly and Fellows-Smith hardly at all. Adcock was more accurate and aggressive, accounting for the two England novices Walker and Barber and finishing with 5-62. England finished with 292 at about 3.15pm on the Friday. It was reckoned to be a reasonable score, but hardly a match-winning one. However, as Brian Johnston kept telling us, the runs were 'on the scoreboard rather than up in the air'. Subba Row and Smith had both reached their half-centuries, and wicketkeeper Jim Parks had put up a reasonable 35.

John Waite wonders what would have been England's total if Peter Heine had been bowling along with Neil Adcock. He sums up Griffin's contribution as follows in a brilliant antithesis: 'Griffin had not once been called for throwing. Nor had he delivered many balls that were dangerous to the batsmen' – something that sums up the South African dilemma about Griffin. He could decide to bowl harmlessly but legally, or try to take wickets and risk the verdict of the umpire. A decade or two later everyone would be talking about a catch-22 situation, but fortunately that particular cliché was not yet with us. The 'horns of a dilemma' was more current in 1960.

It had not been great entertainment, but it was now up to the Springbok batsmen to show what they could do. One, of course, never knows what a good total is until the other side have had a chance to bat as well. South Africa, sadly, fell a little short, and this was, possibly, the key innings of the series. Had they managed to get up to a respectable total and closer to England's, then they might have saved the game, but as everyone who has ever played cricket knows, lack of success is a very infectious thing and failure, almost inevitably, feeds on itself.

John Arlott's command of the English language was legendary, but I wonder how many of his readers would have known the word 'freshet'? The Edgbaston wicket, thanks to occasional 'freshets' of rain, John told us, had some pace to offer to Trueman and Statham as South Africa started their innings. (Bizarrely, in those days, the pitch had to be left uncovered, although it was in order to cover the bowlers' run-ups!) By close of play on the Friday, South Africa were reduced to 114/5, and even that was a recovery from 61/5, as Statham and Trueman threatened to run riot. Cowdrey kept them on, and they gave him all they had, both of them bowling to umbrella fields with loads of fielders in the slips. Neither McGlew nor Goddard looked happy, going for 11 and 10, and then Tony Pithey went lbw to Statham – 'there had been several clear indications that Pithey would be lbw to Statham before he actually was – beaten by both pace and movement', according to John Arlott. Oh, the effect of those 'freshets'!

Often a clear indication that a team is on top comes in their fielding, and a really superb catch was taken by Statham off the bowling of Trueman to dismiss the dangerous Roy McLean. It was a sight to behold. The Lancastrian must have run about 20 or 30 yards from close to the wicket to the long leg boundary to catch a skier, achieving this feat as it dropped over his right shoulder. It was a splendid piece of fielding, and Edgbaston's meagre crowd rose to appreciate such an effort. Apparently, the Australian Keith Miller had shouted in the press box that the odds were 20/1 on the ball. In the context of the game and indeed the series, this was a significant wicket, and McLean's dismissal in the second innings would be even more so.

Previous to this, there had been a certain amount of by-play between McLean and Trueman. Trueman had been getting the better of McLean, but McLean had ridden his luck and on one occasion had hooked Fred's short one to the boundary. This was the equivalent of signing one's own death warrant in cricketing terms, and it may be that a few pleasantries were exchanged between the two men. Be that as it may, Trueman's next ball to McLean was what is called a 'beamer', a waist-high full toss legal in 1960 but punishable nowadays by a no-ball and possibly even the bowler being removed from the attack. It was this ball which McLean sent high in the air and Statham did the needful.

The triumphant Trueman also did for Carlstein, who had not looked happy, trapping him lbw, but eventually wicketkeeper Waite and O'Linn stopped the rot, and without necessarily setting the heather on fire took the score to 114, mainly through prods and nurdles. O'Linn was an interesting character. Born Sydney Olinsky of a Russian Jewish background, he changed his name when he found that his name and race were not always to the liking of everyone in South Africa. Altering his name to O'Linn, however, might have opened him to the only slightly less serious charge (in apartheid South Africa) of being Irish and Catholic, but they seemed more able to cope with that. He was also a footballer and had played for Charlton Athletic a few years previously, as well as cricket for Kent. Oddly and disappointingly in view of his experiences, he does not seem to have come out against the prevailing political system in South Africa.

The Saturday morning was described by John Arlott as 'choppy' and by *Wisden* as 'humid', two almost contradictory adjectives, but for me the problem was the disruption caused by the BBC deciding to put Trooping the Colour on TV for the first hour. Possibly my republican sympathies date from that point, for there are surely few things worse than the sight of soldiers, sovereigns, flags, men saluting other men whom they have known all their lives, and horses when what one really wants is to see Waite and O'Linn battling to save the follow-on. Accused of being boorish and antisocial and told that 'Prince Charles doesn't act like that. He is proud of his mother,' I retired to my room to listen to John Arlott on the radio until such time as the TV resumed the cricket.

Prince Charles was, incidentally, give or take a week or so, the same age as I was. I was always compared unfavourably with this paragon who apparently never spoke back to his mother (that was correct, for he seldom saw her!), never played cricket or football on the street (also correct, for he was never near any street) and always ate what was put in front of him (that one, I didn't know about). It was only in later years that my mother slowly began to realise that perhaps she had done not too bad a job with me after all, in comparison at least with that other post-war baby boomer who really did not turn out to be all that great! In later years, he was not at all nice to 'that lassie' (Princess Diana), according to my mother.

Waite and O'Linn did indeed save the follow-on, but both fell pretty soon afterwards, not to the pace of Statham and Trueman but to the off spin of Raymond Illingworth, described by John Arlott as a 'vastly improved bowler for the experience he gained in the West Indies. He not only wrested a little turn from a somewhat unco-operative wicket but he made the ball float away from the right hander's bat in a puzzling curve.' O'Linn was caught by Cowdrey in the slips after a rush of blood, having saved the follow-on and Waite went to a massive Illingworth off break which pitched outside the off stump and hit the leg. Fellows-Smith was then trapped lbw. It was my first introduction to Ray Illingworth, by no means the best player, but possibly the finest cricketing brain that England produced in the 20th century. His dealings with that other Yorkshireman Geoffrey Boycott are legendary and reflect no real credit on either person, but he is still revered in Leicestershire for his achievements there. He also won the Ashes in Australia in 1970/71 in spite of a 'cool' relationship between himself and people like Colin Cowdrey and EW Swanton!

The South Africans lasted until lunch but not much longer. The still nervous Griffin was bowled by Trueman, having played on, and then Statham, who had fielded magnificently throughout, ran out Tayfield. South Africa, who reached 186, were 106 behind, and in the annoying position of being able to reflect that if just one of their batsmen had got a start – if, for example, McLean had not had that rush of blood to Trueman – things could have been so much better for them. As it was, they were not necessarily out of the game, for England were a man short with Pullar injured, and the pitch had proved receptive to both pace and spin. It was now up to the South African attack, although McGlew sprung an immediate surprise by opening with Adcock and the innocuous medium pace of Goddard, keeping Griffin for later.

Cowdrey opened with Subba Row in place of Pullar, and the innings was off to a sensational start when Cowdrey was out second ball to Adcock, playing on to a highish one. It would be a common form of dismissal as Dexter and Parks both went the same way, Dexter to Adcock and Parks to Griffin, as England struggled. Pullar's incapacitation was now significant, and at the close of play, England's poor score of 89/4 was effectively 89/5, with South Africa well in the game. Illingworth and Smith were struggling in the indifferent light, and the only good stroke play had come from Ted Dexter, who had scored 26. It was, however, a typical Dexter cameo innings of a few good strokes but it did not last as long as the crowd wanted or as England needed. He chopped a shortish ball from Adcock on to his stumps to an audible sigh of disappointment from the crowd.

England thus spent the Sunday rest day some 195 runs ahead, with the better half of their batting now back in the pavilion. It was not yet a commanding or even a winning position, and a lot was clearly going to depend on how England's lower order dealt with the period before lunch on Monday. A lot also depended on Griffin, so far used sparingly by McGlew, who seemed a little afraid that he might be called again for throwing. The debate about his action continued unabated on the Sunday with club cricketers up and down the land making ludicrous statements to the effect that you cannot bowl a ball with a

front-on action like that; it must be a throw in the opinion
of those who believed that emphasis and aggression won
more debates than logical thought did; others stressed
that he was naturally double-jointed and couldn't help
himself. For my part, I demonstrated to my father on the
back green how he bowled. I had taken a liking to Griffin,
and was convinced that he was legal.

It all boiled down to opinion. The nation had now
had a chance to see him on TV, but TV coverage was by
no means as sophisticated as it is now, and proved little
or nothing. The press, for circulation reasons, all said that
he was still 'chucking' at least the occasional ball, if not
every single one. Batsmen, because they had to face him
(or at club level, because they identified with those who
had to do so at Test level), tended to agree, whereas girls
who loved his good looks and gentlemanly demeanour
said that his action was legal, while the middle-aged,
large-breasted, cheerful matrons who made the tea at
cricket clubs were all convinced that the poor, fair-haired,
vulnerable South African was being picked on by the
English establishment. They were possibly not too far
off the mark and a few perceptively and perspicaciously

wondered whether he was paying the price for what Ian Meckiff had done 18 months previously. The opinions that really mattered at that moment, however, were those of umpires John Langridge and Eddie Phillipson who had not yet given any indication that they were unhappy with his current action in this particular game.

Parallel with this debate was the broader one on apartheid. There had been a protest at Edgbaston on the Saturday – a dignified one made up of mainly professional people of both sexes with no disorder and possibly some of the policemen on duty feeling a little redundant, as the protest was confined to standing with placards and giving out leaflets. Everyone has a right to protest, of course – (but, as the protesters said repeatedly, 'Don't try protesting in Sharpeville') – and it was noticeable that a few 'Ban The Bomb' placards were seen as well, allowing the right-wing press to deliver a few tirades about 'scruffy youth' 'with nothing better to do' and 'misplaced utopians' who would in a few years' time 'grow out of it' and vote Conservative. But there were also a good few dog collars of clerics of the Christian Church, and well-dressed ladies and tie-wearing gentlemen. The protest about apartheid was not as large as it should have been, but it was growing. And I loved the placard which read 'Love Cricket, Hate Apartheid!'

This did not stop impassioned arguments. The 'keep politics out of sport' argument is a specious and seductive one and could influence quite a lot of people. But there did seem to be no answer to the argument of why, when black people outnumbered white people in South Africa by such an overwhelming majority, there was not one single black player in their cricket squad. Black people like Gary Sobers and Rohan Kanhai played well enough for the West Indians, and many of them played in English county cricket and in club cricket. Why couldn't black men play for and in South Africa?

There was really no possible answer to this question but, oddly enough, one did hear a few people trying to justify this crazy policy on the grounds that 'the black man' had not developed sufficiently to be able to hold a bat correctly or to know how to spin a ball. I even recall hearing a middle-aged professional gentleman who 'had been in South Africa during the war' (and therefore considered himself the world's expert in this problem!) affirm emphatically that 'the black man's arms are too long to allow him to bowl a cricket ball'. Someone, of a more sensible disposition, then pointed out that 'long arms' had been no disadvantage (indeed they had been a great asset!) to Harold Larwood!

It was at this point when the subject came up in my family that I made the perceptive and possibly even mature (for my tender years) point that, because recently in Great Britain we had had a General Election in which everyone over 21 had voted, why was it not possible to do likewise in South Africa? There was a pause during which one parent marvelled at what an idealistic and intelligent prodigy had been produced, the other one looked at me, sadly and pityingly, and said, 'They are not ready for it yet, I'm afraid!' My father then told me how he had met quite a few South Africans in Second World War and they had all said that 'we have to keep them down'. Otherwise 'they would take over'. But was not that what the other side in the Second World War were saying about Europe? Did Hitler not say that the Jews had to 'kept down', otherwise they might 'take over'? Oh, what a precocious, awkward, persistent little boy I was! And already at the age of 11, showing ominous and dangerous signs of left-wing radicalism!

The Test match resumed on the Monday morning before a very poor crowd. It was now a normal working day for the good people of Birmingham, many of them engaged in building motor cars, clearly the coming growth industry of the 1960s. There was full employment, loads of overtime and not yet the serious labour problems that were to be the curse of the industry for the next couple of decades. The weather alternated between sunshine and showers, some of them very heavy ones, and progress was slow. As England resumed at 89/4, Smith, Illingworth and the luckless Barber (who had had a poor Test match) went cheaply, but Glamorgan's Peter Walker played sensibly and scored 37, which probably played a larger part in the game than the comparatively small number of runs would suggest, and then England's tail wagged.

Trueman and then Statham, by slogging rather than by any sophisticated stroke play, both hit 20s while Walker continued 'sensibly' at the other end. Trueman was particularly severe on Tayfield until he missed a straight one and was bowled, and then Walker gave the still underperforming Griffin his second wicket of the innings by edging him to Goddard. The end of the innings was bizarre, for Pullar came in bravely, wrist in plaster, to support his fellow Lancastrian Brian Statham. Statham clearly saw little point in this, for England now had a lead of over 300, and it was the opinion of most commentators and journalists that he deliberately swung at Griffin and was caught by McLean in order not to expose his injured friend to any hostility from Griffin and Adcock. One would like to know whether 'words' were exchanged in the dressing room between Statham and Cowdrey about this, but the upshot was that England were all out for 203 – not in itself a great score, but setting South Africa 310 to win in a day and a half.

This was a tall order but was by no means beyond a team with the calibre of McLean, Waite, McGlew and Goddard, not to mention the as-yet comparatively unproven talent (at this level) of Fellows-Smith, Carlstein, Pithey and O'Linn. Even Griffin had had a few good scores with the bat the previous winter. All it really required was a good score from at least two of these men. In some ways, it was the big test.

As far as South Africa's bowling was concerned, Griffin would, if he had been on trial for a criminal offence in a Scottish court, have been found 'Not Proven', the verdict which suggests that the accused may well be guilty but the prosecution is short of evidence. He had not been called for a no-ball, and his action had certainly been modified by Alf Gover, but he had definitely been considerably less effective that he might have been.

England, undeniably, had two world-class bowlers in Trueman and Statham, and also now an intelligent spinner in Raymond Illingworth. The loss of Pullar was no longer a problem, for a substitute fielder was allowed, and Pullar never bowled anyway. Dexter was an occasional bowler, but the man who was more anxious than most was Bob Barber, playing his first Test match, and having suffered a fair amount of bad luck so far. The odds were definitely on England, but a South African win was by no means out of the question.

If the weather held good – which was not a certainty – there was more than enough time to win the game for South Africa. There was no point in playing out time. South Africa would be well advised to go for the runs. They could then save the game, if the weather turned nasty or if wickets began to fall. On the other hand, to score over 300 in the fourth innings of the match was considered to be a tall order on a wearing pitch.

But this was clearly a bad Test match for captains. Cowdrey having failed, so too did McGlew, nicking a ball to Jim Parks with a sound that was heard all over the ground, something that says a little about the paucity of the attendance as well. That was after Goddard had gone for a duck, being caught by Walker at backward square leg. Both these wickets went to Statham and, as England's young substitute on for Pullar had dropped another catch off Trueman, the consensus of opinion was that South Africa would not see the night out, let alone get anywhere close to 310.

But Pithey came in and played reasonably well along with Roy McLean for a spell, taking the score a little pedestrianly to 58 before seeming to be in two minds to a delivery from Illingworth and edging the ball on to his stumps, an exceptionally common dismissal in this Test match. It was in some ways a typical innings of Tony Pithey – full of promise, but just as he was looking as if he was beginning to get on top, making a fatal mistake. And yet, he had now shown his ability.

Once more, this began to look like another nail in the South African coffin, but it was the last wicket to fall in the day. Only a massive slice of good luck saved Waite, however, off his very first ball. And it was another 'played on'! He managed to get something on a ball from Illingworth which turned, but the ball trickled towards the base of the stumps, hit them but failed to dislodge the bail. Those close to the action insist that the bail jumped up and landed back down again in its groove, but the crucial thing was that the bail did not fall. Later on, but before he had scored very many, Waite was also dropped by Mike Smith at short leg off Fred Trueman.

Waite and McLean now said 'thank you' to Dame Fortune for their escapes and began to play a few shots quite impressively and South Africa closed the day at 120/3 when they had been, at one point, 58/3. McLean in particular was looking good, and there was no doubt that, as long as he was there, South Africa had a chance of reaching a target which was now less than 200 runs with all the time in the world, or at least a whole day. McLean on form would not need a day to score that amount, and Waite was playing solidly at the other end.

Nevertheless, Birmingham went to bed that night more in confidence of an England victory than otherwise. The bookmakers certainly still favoured England, although with less confidence than they had done at other points in the game. A great deal depended on McLean (68 not out) and Waite, for the rest of the team – Carlstein, O'Linn, Fellows-Smith and Griffin – were as yet inexperienced at this level and Adcock and Tayfield, although all capable of swinging a bat now and again, were hardly even worthy of the description of 'all-rounders'. But in cricket, one never knows.

In fact, the second ball of the final day decided the issue. The first ball was a poor one, patted gently back to Trueman by McLean. The second ball was worse, a veritable long hop, as it appeared, and McLean decided to hook it out of the park. Unfortunately for McLean and South Africa, the ball kept low and McLean was palpably lbw even though Eddie Phillipson by all accounts took a while to make up his mind about it. Those of the small crowd who had turned up might well have packed up their things at this point and gone home. It was a match-defining and possibly even series-defining moment and John Waite lamented the loss of McLean's 'strong shoulders, his steely wrists, keen eyes and fine judgement'.

Waite battled on for 56 not out but there was no one else to support him and the Test match subsided. There was an opportunity for someone to make a name for himself, particularly O'Linn who had of course played for Kent and knew something about English conditions, but it didn't happen, and Trueman, Statham and Illingworth finished up with three wickets each. John Waite uses a striking image to describe his colleagues' hasty departure. He quotes an English writer who says that it was like the 'little Scandinavian rodents, the lemmings, who march *en masse* to the seashore each season when their staple food, the moss, disappears and swim out in their millions until they drown in mass genocide' (I think he means 'suicide' rather than 'genocide').

It was all over by lunch time and England won by exactly 100 runs. It had been a good Test match for England, although their bowling was a lot better than their batting. Their fast men had done well, Illingworth had proved himself once again, and Peter Walker had made an encouraging debut. Cowdrey had had a poor game with the bat, but he had captained the side well and the fielding had been generally quite good. The two negative aspects affected Lancashire players. This was the failure of Bob Barber and the injury to Geoff Pullar.

Only 42,000 had attended the five days and the *Birmingham Daily Post* was clearly worried about the effect this would have on Edgbaston's future as a Test-match venue. TV coverage was blamed, as was the inclement weather and a few even thought that the 'boycott apartheid' brigade had had some effect, but it was also true that neither side had attacked the game as much as they should have. England had won, and although this was enough for some people, it was not really what the cricketing public were wanting. But England and Cowdrey had reason to be happy.

South Africa, on the other hand, had a few wounds to lick as they travelled to Taunton, one of the more pleasant places in England to play cricket. Manager Dudley Nourse made the right noises about the team playing well sometimes and that consistency and reliability were needed. So many batsmen – McGlew, Goddard, Pithey for example – had under-performed, leaving the batting over-dependent on the sometimes flamboyant but reckless McLean. Some of the newcomers had not done as well as they might have, and the issue of Griffin had not been resolved. It seemed that to satisfy the umpires he had to bowl the way that Gover had taught him, which was far less effective. His original action was likely to take wickets but also to have him penalised by the umpires. It would not have been totally surprising if the young man was having a certain 'crisis of confidence', as the current phrase was in 1960.

After this game it was rumoured, not for the first time, that the South Africans had sent home for another player – Peter Heine – to join them and effectively replace Griffin. Another bowler, 6ft 6in Godfrey Lawrence, was also mentioned. It certainly would have made sense to ask for someone else, if Heine refused. These rumours were apparently true, for on 15 June Brian Chapman of the *Daily Mirror* reported that a cable had been sent by Reuters to the effect that 'Mr Arthur Coy, executive member of the South African Board of Control states that a conditional request made by the South African team's tour committee for an additional player, has been refused.

Mr Dudley Nourse, the team manager has been informed. There is no further comment.' And so South Africa were forced to play on with the same 15 players that they had arrived with.

Mr Geoffrey Chubb, president of the South African Cricket Association, was due to arrive by sea some time soon. One member of the party remarked acidly that what was needed was another player, not an administrator. Indeed, it looked for all the world that Mr Chubb was treating himself to a 'jolly'. It would surely not have bankrupted the South African Cricket Association to pay the fare for an extra cricketer as well!

It was certainly a strange business, and clearly there was a great deal of internal politics going on, but many people thought in retrospect that this was the moment when South Africa more or less conceded the series. What was it all about?

First Test Scorecard

ENGLAND FIRST INNINGS

G Pullar c McLean b Goddard	37
MC Cowdrey c Waite b Adcock	3
ER Dexter b Tayfield	52
R Subba Row c Waite b Griffin	56
MJK Smith c Waite b Adcock	54
JM Parks c Waite b Adcock	35
R Illingworth b Tayfield	1
RW Barber lbw b Adcock	5
PM Walker c Goddard b Adcock	9
FS Trueman b Tayfield	11
JB Statham not out	14
Extras	15
TOTAL	292

Fall of wickets: 1/19; 2/80; 3/100; 4/196; 5/225; 6/234; 7/255; 8/262; 9/275

Bowling

Adcock	41.5	14	62	5
Griffin	21	3	61	1
Goddard	33	17	47	1
Tayfield	50	19	93	3
Fellows-Smith	5	1	14	0

SOUTH AFRICA FIRST INNINGS

DJ McGlew c Parks b Trueman	11
TL Goddard c Smith b Statham	10
AJ Pithey lbw Statham	6
RA McLean c Statham b Trueman	21
JHB Waite b Illingworth	58
PR Carlstein lbw b Trueman	4
S O'Linn c Cowdrey b Illingworth	42
JP Fellows-Smith lbw b Illingworth	18
G Griffin b Trueman	6
HJ Tayfield run out	6
NAT Adcock not out	1
Extras	3
TOTAL	186

Fall of wickets: 1/11; 2/21; 3/40; 4/52; 5/61; 6/146; 7/168; 8/179; 9/179

Bowling

Statham	28	8	67	2
Trueman	24.5	4	58	4
Dexter	1	0	4	0
Barber	6	0	26	0
Illingworth	17	11	15	3
Walker	6	1	13	0

ENGLAND SECOND INNINGS

MC Cowdrey b Adcock	0
R Subba Row c Waite b Tayfield	32
ER Dexter b Adcock	26
MJK Smith c O'Linn b Tayfield	28
JM Parks b Griffin	4
R Illingworth c Waite b Adcock	16
RW Barber c McLean b Tayfield	4
PM Walker c Goddard b Griffin	37
FS Trueman b Tayfield	25
JB Statham c McLean b Griffin	22
G Pullar not out	1
Extras	8
TOTAL	203

Fall of wickets: 1/0; 2/42; 3/69; 4/74; 5/112; 6/112; 7/118; 8/163; 9/202

Bowling

Adcock	28	8	57	3
Goddard	10	5	32	0
Tayfield	27	12	62	4
Griffin	21	4	44	3

SOUTH AFRICA SECOND INNINGS

DJ McGlew c Parks b Statham	5
TL Goddard c Walker b Statham	0
AJ Pithey b Illingworth	17
RA McLean lbw b Trueman	68
JHB Waite not out	56
PR Carlstein b Trueman	10
S O'Linn lbw b Barber	12
JP Fellows-Smith lbw b Illingworth	5
G Griffin c Walker b Trueman	14
HJ Tayfield b Illingworth	3
NAT Adcock b Statham	7
Extras	12
TOTAL	209

Fall of wickets: 1/4; 2/5; 3/58; 4/120; 5/132, 6/156; 7/161; 8/167; 9/200

Bowling

Trueman	22	4	58	3
Statham	15	5	41	3
Illingworth	24	6	57	3
Dexter	6	4	4	0
Walker	4	2	8	0
Barber	10	2	29	1

Umpires John Langridge and Eddie Phillipson

CHAPTER 6

LORD'S, NO-BALLS
AND HAT-TRICKS

WOULD TAUNTON and the west country heal the South African wounds and solve the problems? Somerset were next on the itinerary, that most quaint and romantic part of the country which seemed to be almost in a different world from the rest of the United Kingdom, and certainly a million miles away from Birmingham, now undeniably the second city of the Empire – even though by now the word 'Empire' was being replaced by 'Commonwealth'. Once the trip to Somerset had been done, it was onwards to Hampshire at Southampton before London and Lord's.

A positive feature of the tour so far had been how well the South African team had performed against the county sides, and this positive aspect was enhanced by two fine batting performances and easy victories over Somerset and Hampshire. Somerset, never the strongest county side at the best of times, were weakened by injuries, and South Africa gave their four men who had not played in the Test match – Pothecary, Wesley, Duckworth and McKinnon – a game at Taunton in place of Griffin, Pithey, Fellows-Smith and Carlstein. For men who had not been in the Test team, these county games were of utmost importance in that they gave them the opportunity to show their value and potential contribution. One in particular, Atholl McKinnon, the slow left-arm bowler, took full advantage to show what he could do.

The Somerset v South Africans game did not get the headlines in the newspaper. It was knocked off the back pages by the remarkable events at Tunbridge Wells when Kent defeated Worcestershire by an innings and 101 runs and did so all in one day! Finishing a County Championship game in one day was by no means unprecedented but it was rare and had not happened since

1953. On a pitch later described by Kent captain Colin Cowdrey as 'disgraceful', Kent were dismissed for 187, but then David Halfyard took 4-7 and Alan Brown 6-12 to demolish Worcestershire for 25. It cannot be very often that a captain whose team has scored only 187 is in a position to enforce the follow-on, but this is exactly what happened here. Halfyard then had 5-20 as Worcestershire did marginally better the next time round but still could only reach 61! Hardly surprising that Cowdrey was so critical of his own side's pitch! Nevertheless, full marks to Kent and David Halfyard in particular for taking advantage!

It was less dramatic at Taunton, but the South Africans batted first and cheerfully hit 365, one for each day of the year, before close of play on the first day, with McGlew making 73 and O'Linn 69, although it was a minor disappointment that none of the non-Test players sparkled with the bat. The next couple of days were all about good quality spin bowling with Tayfield and McKinnon dismissing the home side twice with McKinnon being particularly impressive with 6-50 and 6-69. For Somerset, Colin McCool and Bill Alley, their sprightly Australian veterans, put up some resistance to entertain the crowd before collapsing to an innings defeat, and the whole three days were a comparative break, an oasis in the middle of controversy and uncertainty, in that quiet and lovely part of the country.

Charles Fortune in *Cricket Overthrown* writes in laudatory style of west-country hospitality, including a game of skittles in a pub in East Lyng in which Somerset gained some revenge for their defeat on the cricket field by winning, while the hero of the hour, the good-natured, burly rugby-playing Atholl McKinnon acted as barman for that lovely, idyllic Wessex evening. One could almost wish that that romantic cameo could have lasted a little longer for the Springboks, because the bells of hell were now beginning to be heard in the distance, ringing for South Africa and Geoff Griffin.

The game against Hampshire at Southampton in sweltering heat was remarkable for many reasons. One was the South African batting on the first and second days which reached the colossal total of 507. And yet it was not all good news for the South Africans. Both Pithey and Duckworth, put in early to give them maximum opportunity, failed. That could not be said about Peter Carlstein who scored an impressive 151, Colin Wesley who hit 84 and was looking good for a century before he was run out, and then Geoff Griffin whose aggressive batting, admittedly against a now weak and demoralised attack, entertained the crowd with three sixes and did a lot to cheer up his many supporters, and of course himself, as he reached 65 not out.

That, however, was as good as it got for Griffin, for in the two Hampshire innings he was called six times for chucking and by both umpires, Jim Parks senior (the father of England's wicketkeeper) and Harry Elliott. Although this was what inevitably made the headlines in the gutter press, and even the more respectable ones, it was irrelevant to the course of the game which the South Africans won by nine wickets, Hampshire putting up a 'miserable performance' according to *Wisden* (which is never afraid to tell the truth) and collapsing to the spin of Tayfield who took 5-66 and 6-78. There was some resistance – Baldry in the first innings with 70, and Horton with 117 and Barnard with 77 in the second which at least staved off an innings defeat, but as far as the rest of the team were concerned, *Wisden*'s brutal assessment was correct. It was indeed a 'miserable performance' and their supporters, who felt they deserved better, were unhappy about it.

Hampshire's moment of glory would occur the following season, 1961, when they won the County Championship for the first time. Their captain would be Colin Ingleby-Mackenzie who very definitely played attacking cricket and got his just rewards. An old-Etonian and amateur of the type that EW Swanton approved of, frequently having the adjective 'swashbuckling' applied to him, he was a larger-than-life character who was known to time declarations so that he could listen to the commentary of a horse race on the radio in the bar, and very soon acquired cult hero status in the county. Sadly, the spectacular success did not last more than the one season, and here in 1960 he had a poor game against Tayfield, being dismissed for 0 and 1. His moment was yet to come.

One would have loved to be privy to the selection process in the South African camp as they made their way to London for the second Test match, which was due to start on 23 June. Would they or would they not play Geoff

Griffin, who had now been called by several umpires? Was it worth the risk when the umpires on duty at Lord's would be Frank Lee and Syd Buller, both reputed to be hard men? The attempt to bring in Peter Heine seemed to have collapsed, but there were still several options open to them if they wanted to avoid what seemed the inevitable trouble. There was another fast bowler in the party called Jim Pothecary. Admittedly he had not yet shown any great form on the tour and was arguably more a fast-medium bowler than a true 'quick', but he might have done well sharing the new ball with Adcock at Lord's (as indeed he was forced to do later in the tour). South Africa might even have played two spinners. In recent matches, McKinnon and Tayfield had won games for them. Lord's was never known as a spinner's wicket, but the tourists in fielding their spinners would certainly have been playing to their strengths. Or there was the other possibility, not apparently considered as yet, of calling up someone else from the many South Africans playing in England.

In the event, Griffin was given the nod. One wonders what the likeable young man had made of the (admittedly half-hearted) attempts to call up Heine. Would this have meant him being 'sacked' from the tour? He was, in all conscience, under enough pressure in the present circumstances, and it was only going to get worse for him.

Alf Gover, writing in the *Sunday Pictorial* on the Sunday before the Test match and BEFORE Griffin had been called in the game against Hampshire, remained convinced that as long as Griffin retained his side-on action, he would not be called. The problem was that his side-on action, as the events at Edgbaston had proved, was a lot less effective and 'bordering on the innocuous', according to some writers. Colin Wesley for Tony Pithey was the only change in the South African side, although Sid O'Linn was to be promoted up the order. It also appears, according to the account given by John Waite, that Griffin was told to 'be himself'. This seems to mean that he was to be encouraged to bowl his natural open-chested action. The thinking was that at least South Africa would now know where they stood, and that in any case, as they were now 0-1 down in the series, some positive thinking was required. 'Appeasement' was no longer an option. Manager Dudley Nourse seems to have decided to dare the umpires to call Griffin.

England opted for three pacemen, introducing Alan Moss of Middlesex (something that Brian Chapman in the *Daily Mirror* had predicted a few days prior) to join the two men from the north, Trueman and Statham. This was at the expense of Bob Barber, a man whose moments of glory for England were yet to come but had clearly not materialised at Edgbaston. Ken Barrington of Surrey, who had been 12th man at Edgbaston, was given a place for the injured Geoff Pullar, although not as an opening batsman, for that spot would be given to Subba Row.

On a dullish day for midsummer, Cowdrey won the toss, and to the surprise of a few commentators who wondered if the conditions might not help the bowlers, chose to bat. But Cowdrey was clearly of the conventional English school of thought which said: 'If you win the toss, bat 80 per cent of the time. The other 20 per cent, think about it first – and then bat!' The England innings would turn out to be the most remarkable and eventful one in the history of Test match cricket.

The first day (Thursday) was badly disrupted by the weather and England finished at 114-2. Griffin was called for a no-ball five times during the day by Frank

Lee. He had been put on to bowl from the Nursery End and captured the wicket of Cowdrey very early, inducing him to drive at a widish one which he mistimed and was caught by McLean at second slip. This raised yet again the question of whether it was wise for Cowdrey to open the innings. He was a far better batsman, it was felt, if he came in later when the shine had gone from the new ball. Dexter then entertained with 55, but the talking point was Griffin and Frank Lee.

The thing which puzzled commentators was that Lee called him five times and passed the others. Yet there seemed to be no difference between the balls that were called and the ones that were passed. Some saw some sinister influence here, as if Lee was under pressure to call him but only did so occasionally; what was more likely was that the poor man who, like most umpires, preferred to quietly enjoy his cricket, was under pressure from his own demons and was suffering the horrors of hell about whether to obey his own conscience or not. Lee knew full well that if he did what his conscience told him, he would ruin and finish this young man's cricketing career. On the other hand, if he didn't call him, he would be given words like 'soft' and 'cowardly' beside his own name in the press, and that might ruin and finish his own umpiring career. His body language made it hard to resist the belief that he would have been far happier at Taunton or Canterbury or Derby in front of a few hundred spectators that day instead of Lord's before thousands and the TV cameras.

John Waite was speaking, one feels, for most of the South African team when he asked pointedly, 'Is this no-balling by Lee inspired, or influenced, by some English official, or officials, behind the glass windows of the Lord's Long Room?' There was nothing that anyone could dignify by the name of 'evidence' to prove this, and of course any attempt to nobble an umpire is a serious offence no matter who does it, but then again it is commonly believed outside the United Kingdom (and even within sometimes) that Britannia when it cannot any longer 'rule the waves' can very subtly and definitely 'waive the rules'.

Not everyone thought that Griffin threw. Australians from a position of neutrality tended to say that his action was fair, notably Keith Miller, the venerable Don Bradman and Richie Benaud, for example, who would lead the Australians the following year. It is not, of course, beyond the bounds of possibility that there was a 'hidden agenda' here as well, with the Aussies possibly fed up of the 'whinging Poms' who blamed all their woes in 1958/59 on Ian Meckiff. The Australians themselves had a point to make about Meckiff's possible inclusion in the squad for 1961.

More surprisingly, Denis Compton, England's star batsman of a decade previously, voiced some support for the South African. Denis, 'the Laughing Cavalier', in spite of his impeccable Middlesex connections, was not always an establishment figure, and had a reputation for eccentricity and even for being a bit of a maverick on occasion. Cynics would of course see a connection here with newspaper circulation figures, but, in any case, the man who mattered the most was Frank Lee. By calling him, Lee had made history in that Griffin was the first man to be called at Lord's in a Test match, and the first member of a touring side to be called in a Test match in England.

It might at this point be profitable to quote the law on the no-ball as it existed. This is Law 26, and although the section on 'drag' or the position of feet is very accurate and precise (and by no means easy for a non-practising cricketer to understand), the stricture on bowling is considerably less so. One may also be surprised to learn that there is nothing in the law to prevent the bowler's-end umpire from calling a no-ball for throwing, although presumably he should be too occupied in watching the feet at the time!

> For a delivery to be fair, the ball must be bowled, not thrown or jerked: if either Umpire be not entirely satisfied of the absolute fairness of a delivery in this respect, he shall call and signal 'No-ball' instantly upon delivery. The Umpire at the Bowler's wicket shall call and signal 'No-ball' if he is not satisfied that at the instant of delivery, the Bowler has at least part of one foot behind the Bowling crease and within the Return crease, and not touching or grounded over either crease.

The miserable weather that obtained that day had John Waite descending or ascending to poetic descriptions of the scene, talking about a London day 'which, for the most part, made Lord's Cricket Ground resemble a mist-veiled river in midwinter, a river peopled, deserted and re-peopled by ghostlike, flannelled figures in unreal procession'. There was indeed something very Dickensian about the whole thing.

The following day, Friday, history was bizarrely made in several ways. England built steadily, Subba Row scoring 90, MJK Smith 99 and Peter Walker 52 on a rain-disrupted day, but the real drama was elsewhere than in the England batting. Griffin bowled off and on throughout the day but always at the Nursery End. He was not called by Lee, and according to Charles Fortune, Lee did not even seem interested. 'Lee's attitude looked precisely that of one who had fully registered his verdict and saw no point thereafter in re-stating his case. Since someone had to bowl and since Griffin was causing no batsman any particular difficulty, there the matter might as well rest. All of which seemed entirely civilized and logical.'

But things suddenly changed after lunch. Griffin's first over saw him no-balled twice and it would have been a 'hat-trick' if Buller had not beaten Lee to it to call him for 'drag'. It was difficult not to detect a certain amount of 'nobbling' here as if someone from the MCC had 'had a word' with Lee at the lunch interval. The malign influence of GOB Allen (Gubby Allen) currently chairman of the England Selectors, was widely suspected of being at work here, especially when it was admitted that he and South African manager Dudley Nourse had already crossed swords on this issue.

Gubby Allen was never a very popular character. To his credit there was the part he had played in the 1932/33 tour of Australia when he refused to play along with Douglas Jardine's bodyline policy (for which he was marginalised and more or less shunned by Jardine on the tour) but, against that, there was widespread evidence of his authoritarianism and desire to retain the amateur v professional distinction. The stories that he was the illegitimate son of 'Plum' Warner are probably without foundation, but there is no doubt that he owed his rise to power to not a little nepotism and favouritism. He was certainly an inveterate snob, but on the other hand he was a great believer in the traditional values of cricket – and for this he deserves some credit. If, however, he had

had anything to do with the so-called 'nobbling' of the umpires, it becomes a very serious matter.

Rain soon intervened that Friday afternoon, but when play resumed, England were continuing their slow but solid progress as close of play approached. Annoyingly, it was not on TV – at this time of year it had to share airtime with tennis coverage at Wimbledon – but it was on the radio. Griffin's bowling had been poor but he was now bowling to MJK Smith who was on 97 and soon nudged a two to bring him up to 99 for the last ball of Griffin's over. Smith's innings, belaboured though it might have been, would have deserved a century but it was not to be. Griffin bowled a ball outside the off stump, Smith went for it and could only snick it to Waite, out for 99. Griffin would have been forgiven for glancing at the umpire to see if he had been called for no-ball again, but Smith stalked off shaking his head and Griffin had at least one wicket to make up for his other misfortunes. To his credit, Smith never blamed his ill luck on 'throwing', at least not in public.

That was the end of the over, and by the time that Griffin came on to bowl the next one, Peter Walker, who had scored an impressive 52, was facing. Concentration late in the day was now a problem, however, for he played back to Griffin, missed and was bowled. Out came Freddie Trueman, blissfully unaware that Griffin was on a hat-trick and glowering at the fielders, as was his wont. Clearly he fancied a few lusty blows to bring the score, already on a healthy 360, up to nearer 400. He swung wildly at Griffin and was bowled. Trueman was unhappy, but Griffin did not show any great emotion in the way that the rest of his team-mates, Adcock in particular, did. Possibly it may be that Griffin himself did not realise that it was a hat-trick! To his already remarkable day for the wrong reasons, he had now added another distinction, this time for the right reasons, that of being the first man to take a hat-trick in a Test match at Lord's. And all on that same crazy day of Friday, 24 June 1960!

A few years later at secondary school when my English teacher, a ferocious spinster, told me that an oxymoron was the apposition of two apparently contradictory words like 'humiliating victory' or a 'glorious defeat' or a 'clever fool' or a 'benevolent despot', I kept thinking of Geoff Griffin on 24 June 1960. For this young faired-haired man who was now undeniably my hero, that day was an oxymoron. It was either a 'disastrous triumph' or a 'victorious catastrophe'. As Macbeth might have put it, 'So fair and foul a day I have not seen.'

But all literary references must yield to the historical parallel unearthed by South African wicketkeeper John Waite whose knowledge of African history is mightily impressive and clearly puts to shame all the Oxford academics who were known to take a day off their Classical researches and teachings for the purpose of coming in to London for a spot of cricket at Lord's.

'The young Zululander, who had been born in Eshowe close to the battle kraal of Chaka Zulu, had enjoyed the same sweet revenge that Chaka's successor, Dingaan, tasted in the early 19th century. And revenge is sweet even in the teachings of Zulu gods!' I bet it was, for the young man whose persecution in the English press was ongoing and relentless.

Cowdrey declared overnight at 362/8. It is important to state that although South Africa had had a terrible day, they were not necessarily as yet out of this Test match. Three days remained, and although the England score was respectable, it was no more than that and it was not out of the question that their total could be equalled or even beaten. The game could certainly, at that point, have been saved. The England total was not gigantic. It is something that must be borne in mind when one analyses the reasons for South Africa's defeat. The no-balling of Griffin was emphatically not the only, or even the main, reason for South Africa's dismal defeat, other than possibly in the psychological aspect of all that had gone on, and the effect it had on everyone. On this sultry Saturday, however, the spotlight and the immediate pressure was temporarily off Griffin.

The weather had improved, even though a thunderstorm would severely curtail the afternoon session, and a large crowd of 27,000 was there. It was, after all, the Saturday of the Lord's Test match in midsummer, and very much a society occasion with the well-dressed appearing with their wicker picnic baskets, and horsey young women loudly saying things like 'sooper' and 'yah', while the working classes from Lewisham and Islington with their sandwiches in paper bags headed towards the parts of the ground where the seating was free. They were entitled to expect to see some sort of South African fightback with some fine stroke-play from the likes of McGlew, Goddard and in particular McLean. The morning newspapers were of course, as John Waite commented in *Perchance to Bowl*, 'all about Griffin, Griffin and nothing but Griffin' with headlines like 'Chucker boy takes hat-trick' and 'the illegitimate threesome' in the popular press, as if some unmarried mother had given birth to triplets, and less sensational (but no less committed) headlines in newspapers like the *Daily Telegraph* to the effect that more effective action would have to be taken against illegal deliveries.

There was no complicated or technical reason for South Africa's collapse. Only up to a point can we make excuses and talk about the previous day's seismic happenings. The real reasons were quite simply poor batting and good bowling, the usual reasons in fact for batting collapses, however much one talks about surfaces, wickets, tracks and vague, intangible concepts like 'variable bounce'. There was also the 'ridge' at Lord's which was made much of by England the next year to explain their defeat at the hands of Australia. But it is often just sheer panic that sets in to the batting side after a few early bowling successes.

Brian Statham, bowling from the Nursery End (or for those who were watching on TV, towards the cameras, for the coverage was only from one end in 1960) took 6-63, showing the benefits of accuracy, line and length. He was backed up by Alan Moss bowling on his own pitch and taking 4-35, and also by some brilliant catching and fielding by wicketkeeper Jim Parks and slip fielder Colin Cowdrey in particular. Trueman missed out on the feast of wickets, but still could not be accused of bowling badly. As always, however, it was not easy for him to put a smile on his face when he was (temporarily) not the centre of attention.

For South Africa, it was doubly vexatious, for none of their players could really claim to have got 'a brute of a ball' on immediate arrival at the crease. They all got started. Eight out of the 11 managed to reach double figures, but only one, Jonathan Fellows-Smith, reached the 20s. McGlew, Goddard, McLean and Waite all perished to Statham when they had given the impression of being equal to the situation. McGlew, to his credit, did not make a fuss about it at the time, but claimed later that Statham's fast ball had hit his bat first before the pad but umpire Buller had given him out.

Griffin came out to bat at number ten, and met with a mixed reception. Some booed, some gave him a cheer, but certainly the social chit-chat about who was having an affair with whom in the office died down, as everyone took their opportunity to look at the man who was currently, for good reason or bad, dominating world cricket. Ironically, when facing Statham, there was a call of 'no-ball' – and everyone thought that one of the umpires was playing a very cruel joke – but it was for drag. When Griffin was bowled by Statham for 5, South Africa were all out for a paltry 152 and well below the follow-on target.

Cowdrey might have given his bowlers a rest, but decided to go for the throat and enforce the follow-on. Surely the South Africans had to do better this time! Storm clouds, in more senses than one, were gathering as McGlew and Goddard came to the crease. McGlew perished cheaply again for 17, bowled almost inevitably by Statham, and when the rains came down 90 minutes before the scheduled close, South Africa were 34-1. Again, one really good innings from one of their batsmen, backed up by a few half-decent scores and a few more rain showers might just have saved the day for the Springboks, but the button of self-destruction had now been well and truly pressed. The air of depression was palpable and almost tangible.

Once again, on the Monday, South Africa batted like a team who knew they were beaten. Another figure of speech that my learned but 'difficult' English teacher told me was a 'prolepsis', the anticipation of something before it actually happened like 'the doomed army marched to destruction'. This was definitely what happened here with even the primitive TV cameras able to pick up the body language of the South Africans walking to the wicket. They were like men going to the dentist. This time Trueman had a couple of wickets, but it was mainly Statham again, and although Fellows-Smith and Wesley put up a little resistance, the end came soon after lunch with South Africa all out for 135 and losing by an innings and 73 runs. It has to go down as one of their worst-ever defeats. It was abject surrender.

It would have been better if things had just stopped there and then, and everyone had gone home. But the snag was that the Queen was due to arrive later in the afternoon, and to fill in the time and to entertain the paltry crowd, they decided to have an 'exhibition match', a primeval T20 game, if you like. There is evidence to suggest that quite a few of the players on both sides were less than 100 per cent happy about this event, variously described as a 'funfare', a 'carnival' a 'mockery' and certainly 'not real cricket', but the game went ahead, and actually South Africa won, something that earned them even a few cheers from the Lord's crowd!

But it was the action of the umpires that attracted attention. Whether they were happy about this game going ahead or not, we don't know, but they gave one of the worst displays of pomposity, officiousness and sheer lack of humour that one is ever likely to see on a cricket field. They might easily have agreed that as this was a show game, Griffin could bowl his normal action. But Sid Buller, who had previously shown a few signs of wanting in on the action, now found himself at square leg to Griffin.

Griffin bowled a couple off a short run. A wise umpire might have decided that as Griffin was making an effort, to turn a Nelsonian blind eye to the possibility he may just have had a slightly bent arm. But Buller, clearly one of the type of umpire sadly all too familiar at local level, with no sense of humour and unaware of the unwritten Law 47 that 'the umpire at all times must act with common sense', ostentatiously crossed to point and back again to get a better view. In fact, he had already made up his mind. He called the third, fourth and fifth balls, a long discussion took place between McGlew and Buller with Lee also wandering across to join in, Griffin then decided to bowl underarm lobs just to finish the over, and was promptly no-balled by Lee for failing to tell him that he was changing to underarm! If it had not been so serious for young Griffin, this performance would not have been out of place in a Christmas pantomime. The cause of umpiring was done no favours that day.

There was, of course, in 1960, nothing in the laws to prevent the bowler bowling underarm as long as he told the umpire and batsman first. That law was only changed after Trevor Chapple's notorious underarm 'grubber' or 'moosey crawler' in 1981 to prevent a New Zealand batsman hitting a six. But in 1960 it was the attitude and the demeanour of the umpires that caused the problem.

There were other 'takes' on Buller as well. Bob Barber, for example, who played (poorly) in the first Test match and was 12th man in the second, has this to say about Buller in his foreword to a book called *The Altham-Bradman Letters*, written by Robin Brodhurst: 'Players and umpires who had seen Griffin bowl were generally of the view that he threw. I suspect my friend Jackie McGlew also had reservations. At this period umpires, their livelihoods dependent upon county captains' assessments, were mostly too afraid to stand up and be counted. Griffin was shielded from umpire Syd Buller. Perhaps Jackie thought he would not be no-balled in a fun game, so he bowled Griffin with Syd at square leg. Syd was regarded as the best umpire in England. Additionally, his integrity was rock solid. After the match, Jackie asked for Syd to be removed from the list of Test match umpires county captains produced. A quorum of county captains … were told that the rules stipulated that a request by a visiting captain must be acceded to. Syd was removed for doing what he believed was correct. He was undoubtedly very hurt to be withdrawn from the remaining Tests that summer. I understand he was paid his full fee for standing in the

Tests that summer and he was subsequently reappointed to the Test panel.' Griffin was thus clearly not the only casualty of the affair.

However that may be, South Africa won the meaningless exhibition or show game, the players met the Queen (in 1960 a pretty young lady with no obvious interest in the game of cricket) and everyone eventually went home after some of the most remarkable days in Test match history, and a game from which the only people who emerged with any real credit were Brian Statham and possibly some of the English batsmen, Mike Smith and Raman Subba Row in particular. Griffin, a hat-trick hero, always retained his dignity and his apparently phlegmatic demeanour earned everyone's respect and even admiration.

The South Africans had every right to be ashamed for themselves for their awful batting, the umpires did a lot to bring the game into disrepute, and the politicians, journalists and officials of both sides hardly helped, even though all of them talked impressively about 'the good of the game', as if they were the sole representatives of cricket's probity and honour. It was a low point in the season at the time when the midsummer weather was good (sometimes!) and cricket should have been enjoyed.

John Arlott also makes the point that he feels that South Africa's selection of Griffin was utterly cynical, as if they were prepared to see him called six or seven times per day in return for the wickets that he would take when he was not called. He likens this to a football team conceding a free kick to break up the opposition's attack.

Second Test Scorecard

ENGLAND FIRST INNINGS

MC Cowdrey c McLean b Griffin	4
R Subba Row lbw b Adcock	90
ER Dexter c McLean b Adcock	56
KF Barrington lbw b Goddard	24
MJK Smith c Waite b Griffin	99
JM Parks c Fellows-Smith b Adcock	3
PM Walker b Griffin	52
R Illingworth not out	0
FS Trueman b Griffin	0
JB Statham not out	2
AE Moss did not bat	
Extras	32
TOTAL	362/8

Fall of wickets: 1/7; 2/103; 3/165; 4/220; 5/227; 6/347; 7/360; 8/360

Bowling

Adcock	36	11	70	3
Griffin	30	7	87	4
Goddard	31	6	96	1
Tayfield	26	9	64	0
Fellows-Smith	5	0	13	0

SOUTH AFRICA FIRST INNINGS

DJ McGlew lbw b Statham	15
TL Goddard b Statham	19
S O'Linn c Walker b Moss	18
RA McLean c Cowdrey b Statham	15
JHB Waite c Parks b Statham	3
PR Carlstein c Cowdrey b Moss	12
C Wesley c Parks b Statham	11
JP Fellows-Smith c Parks b Moss	29
HJ Tayfield c Smith b Moss	12
G Griffin b Statham	5
NAT Adcock not out	8
Extras	5
TOTAL	152

Fall of wickets: 1/33; 2/48; 3/56; 4/69; 5/78; 6/88; 7/112; 8/132; 9/138

Bowling

Statham	20	5	63	6
Trueman	13	2	49	0
Moss	10.3	0	35	4

SOUTH AFRICA SECOND INNINGS (following on)

DJ McGlew b Statham	17
TL Goddard c Parks b Statham	24
S O'Linn lbw b Trueman	8
RA McLean c Parks b Trueman	13
JHB Waite lbw b Statham	0
PR Carlstein c Parks b Moss	6
C Wesley b Dexter	35
JP Fellows-Smith not out	27
HJ Tayfield b Dexter	4
G Griffin b Statham	0
NAT Adcock b Statham	2
Extras	1
TOTAL	137

Fall of wickets: 1/26; 2/49; 3/49; 4/50; 5/63; 6/72; 7/126; 8/132; 9/133

Bowling

Statham	21	6	34	5
Trueman	17	5	44	2
Moss	14	1	41	1
Illingworth	1	1	0	0
Dexter	4	0	17	2

One might have felt that the month of June had already visited enough horrors on the South Africans but there was still a final humiliation awaiting them in Bristol. It was a green-top wicket, but that is no excuse, for good teams can play better on any pitch than poorer ones can. The tourists, however, were now demoralised with quite a few of them clearly pining for home – and the tour still had a couple of months to run! But once more it was necessary to repair to the west country, this time to take on Gloucestershire.

McGlew, Griffin, McLean and Fellows-Smith sat this one out, and Goddard captained the side for a game that lasted little longer than half its scheduled time. The South Africans were shot out for 115, with Tayfield's 24 being the top score. But then the South African bowlers began to enjoy themselves and dismissed Gloucestershire for 81, giving themselves a lead of 35. A little sensible batting seemed called for now in the second innings, but they collapsed to Dennis A'Court and David Smith for 49, their lowest score in England since 1912 and only Peter Carlstein showed the slightest resistance. The final innings of the game was at least exciting, but just as short-lived as the other three, and Gloucestershire edged home with three wickets to spare, the tourists having made the fatal error of dropping Nicholls who finished the game with 35 not out, by some distance the best individual score of the whole game! Gloucestershire supporters were happy with their side's performance but entitled to feel short-changed by the lack of cricket! The South Africans at least enjoyed their brief stay in Bristol, seeing among other things the remarkable Clifton Suspension Bridge and wondering at the genius of Isambard Kingdom Brunel.

For at least the third time on the tour, the possibility of sending for Peter Heine was raised. This time, the balance of evidence was that another cable was sent, but the request was not fulfilled. Whether the South African Cricket Board decided this, or whether Heine himself (for perfectly understandable reasons) refused is not clear in the welter of conflicting and unsubstantiated claims, but the upshot was that the 15 men remained. Griffin himself, now out of the tour as a bowler, did not go home, but stayed on as a batsman and fielder, roles which he accepted with dignity, enthusiasm and not without success.

Although I was sorry for Geoff Griffin, there were other things on my mind. Late June saw my last few days at primary school, and 1960 was also World Refugee Year. In honour of this, and with me being now a senior and even venerable pupil, I took part in a couple of things, both of which had an effect on me. One was an introduction to amateur dramatics – a silly but imaginative play in which I was the King of Hearts, and had to deal with a problem caused by the Knave stealing some tarts and the state visit of the King and Queen of Spades. The girl who played the Queen of Hearts I fell in love with (such things happen quite a lot on the professional stage, they tell me!) but as was often sadly the case, the feelings were not reciprocated. I learned painfully at that point the meaning of 'unrequited love'.

But there was also a quiz for which I was chosen to represent my school. I wasn't very good at my nursery rhymes, mixing up Little Bo Peep and Little Boy Blue, but I then quietened the audience by answering that Abraham Lincoln was the American president shot in a theatre, and really brought the house down by telling them that Kimberley in South Africa was famous for diamonds.

And how did I know that? A few days previously on the television, Brian Johnston had mentioned one of the South African cricketers (annoyingly I can't remember which one) having some vague connection with Kimberley 'and the sparklers' as Brian put it.

And there was also something else at the end of June which impinged on my consciousness – and that was tennis. Once again, one can blame the television for that. Tennis never took over my life in the way that cricket did – indeed there were times when it was an absolute pest and got in the way of cricket – but I did learn a little about the game.

No one told me what 'set point' or 'match point' meant though, until the Wimbledon Men's Singles Final, when Neale Fraser beat Rod Laver, and just before he did so, Dan Maskell said, 'Match point, in fact Championship point.' Ah! It all made sense now! I also discovered that 'love' in tennis had nothing to do with the back seat in the pictures on a Saturday night or what the woman down the road (less respectably) did with a widower when her own husband was working on the night shift. It was actually the French word for an egg! I also worked out that Maria

Bueno, had she been English or Scottish, would have been known as Mary Good.

Such things exercised my mind in these exciting and awakening days of my life, but for the South Africans there was now a trip to Old Trafford, Manchester, followed by the third Test match at Trent Bridge. They cannot have approached them with any kind of enthusiasm, relish or optimism.

CHAPTER SEVEN

TRENT BRIDGE
AND OLD TRAFFORD

THE WOUNDED South Africans now made their way to Manchester to play Lancashire. Old Trafford, in some ways the best and most historic ground in England, can be a desolate place when the weather is bleak. Manchester was also a city, in 1960, which it would have been difficult to visit without being aware of what had happened to the men from the other Old Trafford in February 1958. This was, of course, the fine Manchester United team destroyed in the snows of the dreadful Munich air disaster. The air of grief was still tangible and the rebuilding process was a slow one – but it would happen.

The cricket Old Trafford (only a short and walkable distance away from the footballing one), although notorious and indeed the butt of jokes for its ability to attract rain, tends to be a place where things happen, notably the virtuoso performance of Jim Laker in 1956 who took 'full wickets' (i.e. all ten) in Australia's second innings after taking nine in the first. In 1961, there would be a scarcely less memorable Test match with Richie Benaud spinning Australia to victory from an almost impossible position.

The fine pavilion on the deep-midwicket boundary (as it then was) is a wonderful sight when full of people, but on this Saturday, although play was continuous more or less all day, the weather was inhospitable and the South Africans fielded a weakened side without Adcock, Pithey, Carlstein and Wesley. Funnily enough, Griffin played but only as a fielder and a batsman. It now seemed to have been decided that he would not bowl again on this tour.

The cricket world was still reeling from the effects of Lord's. The South Africans may have been able to shelter behind the Griffin fiasco, but they also had to reckon with the undeniable fact that Griffin had had nothing to do with their batting shortcomings, which were patent and visible to all. Both the Edgbaston and the Lord's Tests could have and should have been saved with a little more application and determination in their batting. However, these games had gone, and the future now had to be faced. It was time to give others a chance.

Thus, we had Pothecary and Goddard opening the attack, never likely to strike terror into anyone's heart, and although Pothecary (who had developed a fondness for potatoes during this tour, so much so that his nickname was now 'Spud'!), had a couple of early successes, Lancashire ran riot and were able to declare at 351/6 well before close of play, with Ken Grieves and Jack Bond having taken centuries off an extremely depleted attack. The depressing part of it all was that even the spinners, Tayfield and McKinnon, were put to the sword. It was impossible not to shed a metaphorical tear or two for Geoff Griffin who fielded conscientiously, ignoring the cries of the ignorant (in that large, echoing stadium with a sparse crowd, one heard everything that was said), but he must have wished that he had been able to bowl.

He was, however, able to bat and, along with Roy McLean, managed to knock up 65 not out and to save the follow-on. Some of his strokes were excellent, his two sixes and ten fours eliciting a round of applause from the meagre Old Trafford crowd. Perhaps he might be in the Test team after all – as a batsman! Indeed, they could have done worse. The batting in the first innings in particular at Trent Bridge turned out to be particularly awful, and Griffin might just have put up some sort of resistance.

With the follow-on saved at Old Trafford and Lancashire batting again, rain came early on the Tuesday morning, and no one showed any sign of unhappiness as the game was abandoned at an early stage, and the South Africans set off south to Nottingham for another Test match. They cannot really have been looking forward to it. They had already been well beaten twice, even though there had been glimmers that they might have done better at certain points, but even if one ignored the Griffin affair (more or less impossible in the continuing media maelstrom), there was no getting away from the fact that both Tests had been lost with barely a whimper of resistance in the latter part of the games. They were up against a very strong England side.

England, not surprisingly, kept the same team that had played at Lord's, whereas South Africa, who might have decided that the time was ripe to make a few changes, did not do so apart from the one that was virtually forced on them, namely Pothecary for Griffin. Griffin thus joined Duckworth, Pithey and McKinnon among the spectators. There was a strong school of thought which said that South Africa should gamble with two spinners, for McKinnon had done well in the county games, and the fourth Test match was to be played at Old Trafford in what looked likely to be damp conditions. Trent Bridge, however, was a game that South Africa simply had to win if they were to stay in the series. Even a draw would mean that they could not win the series, and a defeat would mean that England would hold an impregnable 3-0 lead. Better then to put their best foot forward, it was suggested, and deploy their spinners. The South Africans thought otherwise.

The sports pages of that morning's newspapers were full of speculation about what might happen at Trent Bridge, but the front pages were full of the death of Nye Bevan, one of the foremost politicians of the day and the man who is deservedly given the credit for the creation of Labour's greatest achievement, the National Health Service. In time, particularly 60 years after 1960 at the time of the 2020/21 coronavirus pandemic, people came to realise just what an achievement this was. In 1960, full credit was not always given for what Nye had done, and his name was almost a dirty word in some households, but the time would come when people learned to appreciate him. My family had already done so, with both my father and grandfather (they did not always agree) united in respectful reverence for the Welshman with the Scottish wife.

At Trent Bridge, England won the toss yet again and chose to bat. By end of the first day, it could be argued that with England 242/7, South Africa had the better of things. The bowling was steady but not spectacular, and the same could be said of the English batting. Cowdrey, whether he was a natural opening batsman or not, opened and scored 67 and Barrington 80, and with Illingworth and Walker once again showing their ability to amass late-order runs, England eked out the innings to nearly lunchtime on the Friday and eventually reached 287. For the tourists, although Adcock was for once disappointing, Goddard was the pick of the bowling with 5-80.

Once again, as at Lord's, it must be emphasised that 287 was a good total – but it wasn't a great one. South Africa had not been batted out of the game. Indeed, Trevor Goddard with his excellent figures and to a lesser extent Hugh Tayfield with 3-58, had shown the value of sensible bowling. The wicket was fair for both sides. There could be no excuse for what happened next. England's bowlers Statham, Trueman and Moss were good and the fielding and catching were also very supportive, but South Africa's batting simply surrendered in a way which caused dreadful distress to their supporters.

Charles Fortune in *Cricket Overthrown* has this to say on the unfortunate (for a South African) events of that Friday afternoon on 8 July 1960, when their paltry total of 88 was their lowest since 1924 and the lowest ever in any Test match at Trent Bridge.

I don't pretend to know the reasons, but I do know something of the frame of mind possessing the South Africans at the time. The team was completely on edge – I suppose the psychiatrists would have classified a number of them as emotionally disturbed. That complaint varied with different members from plain 'bloody mindedness' to stark bewilderment. From the day the South Africans flew into England they had been acutely aware that their very presence in England had given offence to a minority, but not an inconsiderable number, of the people living in England. Always they were on guard to avoid any single act or expression of opinion that might accentuate what ill-will towards South Africa there existed in England. I knew something of this myself. My mail had brought dozens of abusive letters within the first week of my starting to broadcast the cricket over BBC transmissions for listeners in England. Almost without exception these were very anonymous letters and couched in terms that varied from the arrogant to the crude. Every cricket commentator who broadcasts regularly gets letters that are rude and abusive. These were different. It was not my commentaries that gave rise to antagonism but the very fact that I lived in South Africa and accompanied the touring team. I received more than 50 letters of this sort. Letters in plenty of the same brand had flowed in for the players.

Let me add at once, it is not only in England that these letters come to men on cricket tours. By far the most scurrilous letter I have ever encountered was one sent from the Eastern Cape Province to a BBC commentator when he was with an MCC tour in South Africa. That particular letter, like the ones received by us in England, vilified the country we represented and ourselves only indirectly. Commentators get case-hardened to these occupational hazards. But young cricketers, more especially those who have still to make their mark, take such tirades to heart. For any young man, it is a terrifying experience to be a figure much in the public eye, yet feeling he is unwanted.

The Griffin business still smouldered. Defeat at Bristol and a poor performance at Manchester had sapped still further what confidence in themselves many of the players still retained. Manager and captain were in their mutual relations rapidly approaching what might be termed 'the point of no return'. Nor was the dressing-down which the whole team got on the afternoon preceding the Test the most tactful way of ensuring that the team would take the field at Trent Bridge bursting with self-esteem.

This is a fascinating account of the morale of an unsuccessful touring team breaking down under pressure – particularly the deterioration in the relationships between Nourse and McGlew – but there are several things that Fortune says which will simply not pass muster, in particular the hate mail. In the first place, as he admits himself, it is a sad part of public life that one is liable to get cowardly abuse like this. It should of course be ignored, and Mr Fortune should be glad he is not around 60 years later when 'social media' carries abuse and hate mail to a newer and higher level of filth, vitriol and sheer bile. But he does avoid the real issue here. He talks about 'ill-will towards South Africa', for example. He does not say why there is such ill-will, or address himself to why there is such a problem. In short, he does not mention words like 'apartheid' or 'Sharpeville'.

It would not have been beyond the bounds of reason for the touring squad to issue a statement deploring the Sharpeville massacre, dissociating themselves from it and vowing to work towards, in the future, the gradual integration of other races into cricket in South Africa. Some might have thought this disloyal, but of course it is always possible to be critical of one's government without being disloyal to one's country. It would have made the world sit up and take notice, and would have been a major embarrassment to their government. It would have delivered a 'bloody nose' to the 'keep politics out of sport' brigade with their facile statements that 'they are here to play cricket' and 'let politicians deal with their own problems', etc. Most importantly, it might have brought forward the ideal of racial integration by many years. Sadly, this did not happen, and one is left with the inescapable but deplorable conclusion that apartheid was supported by the South African cricketers. Why was this the case?

And yet there was a basic contradiction here which, at the age of 11, I could not handle, and still cannot handle some 60 years later. How could such nice men (from all appearances) and such good cricketers possibly represent such an evil concept as something which was not all that far short of slavery? I had already learned at school about the Spartan Helots in Ancient Greece. The Helots were the original inhabitants of the area of Greece where Sparta was (Messenia and Laconia) and they were enslaved by the invading Dorians Greeks who settled in Sparta. Being precocious, I ventured to suggest that the British and the Dutch who went to southern Africa did something by no means dissimilar. The parallel was quite striking. The original inhabitants had their own culture and it was dismantled by the invaders. Was that not what happened to the black South Africans?

And then we found out why the Spartans had to be tough. They were out-populated by the Helots who therefore had to be controlled and held to task. Did this not also ring bells when one looked at South Africa? Some people immediately put me down as a dangerous young radical.

Thank heavens I stayed to be a dangerous middle-aged and now a dangerous old radical!

And as for Charles Fortune saying that it was hate mail which led to 88 all out, even the most naïve of his readers can surely see that this is rubbish. It will simply not do. The South Africans had actually played quite well against most of the counties, and one or two players had given many fine performances. But when things go badly, however, they keep going badly unless someone shows a great deal of mental strength. That seemed to be lacking, and low scores became 'infectious', as happens in all cricketing collapses. Experienced players like McLean, Goddard and McGlew let themselves down by lack of application and sheer mental weakness. There is some excuse for Waite, who was injured in England's innings and batted at number eight. Few other excuses are admissible with an honourable exception in the case of Jonathan Fellows-Smith, who managed 31 not out through a little application and determination. Things did not really need to be as bad as 88 all out.

We are, of course, in danger of not saying enough about England's performance in the field. It was one of England's finest days both with the ball and in their fielding. Walker, for example, took two great catches and Dexter had a brilliant run out to dispose of Goddard, but more than that, England's body language was good. They wanted to be there, they supported each other, they respected Colin Cowdrey their captain, and they behaved like proper sportsmen. There may have been – in fact there is little doubt that there were – a few differences in the dressing room. But such differences stayed there. Trueman took five wickets, McGlew and O'Linn at the start and three tailenders at the end. England now EXPECTED to win – and it is remarkable in sport how often one gets what one expects.

The Trent Bridge ground had seldom seen anything like this before. The innings did not last three hours and when the Springboks followed on at 4.45pm on the Friday it was widely believed that the match would not last to the Saturday. This would have led to a tremendous loss of revenue, and although it was fanciful and even scurrilous to suggest that England were under a little pressure to 'ease up' and make sure that the game did not finish on the Friday night, there was little doubt that a lot of people, including the schedulers of TV programmes on the BBC, were delighted when bad light brought about a premature close an hour early with South Africa on 34/3.

This ensured that some cricket would be played on Saturday, but the premature close on Friday saw Goddard, McLean and Fellows-Smith sitting in the pavilion reflecting yet again on the ways of the world, and in the case of Goddard and McLean, wondering how they had managed to get out twice in a day. The young and inexperienced Fellows-Smith had been the not-out batsman in the first innings, but even he must have been bewildered by it all.

There was a certain amount of whinging from the South Africans. McLean in particular, wasn't happy about the decision given against him, and moaned on about bad light and how they had been forced to bat on when an appeal had been granted to England the day before. Again, as an excuse, this simply will not do. Such judgements and decisions on the part of the umpires are never easy and one has to sympathise with them, but it must also be pointed out that 'appeals against the light' seldom have any support from the spectators who have paid good money to see cricket, rather than to see players walking off because of bad light. If McLean was 'in a fury of indignation' (as was reported) when he came out to bat, it is to be hoped that his anger was directed at himself and his team-mates for their awful first innings performance rather than the wicked umpires who were forcing them to play cricket! The umpires were criticised (and rightly) for their role in the Griffin affair; they are exonerated from criticism here.

John Arlott hit hard in his book *Cricket on Trial*. 'Trueman and Statham bowled magnificently today, but it must be said that the South Africans did not bat very well. They seem a dispirited side. The no-balling of Griffin and then the defeat by Gloucester seem to have depressed them so that they do not seem to compensate for their technical deficiencies by determination.' Concepts like mental strength and positive attitude were clearly lacking.

The crowd for the normally money-spinning Saturday was given as 11,000. This was poor compared with other Test match Saturdays at Trent Bridge in the past, but considering that there was still every prospect of the game finishing by lunchtime, 11,000 was not a bad

188

turnout. In fact, South Africa fought back. Jackie McGlew, whose batting had been miserable so far in the Test series, suddenly found form, with strong, if occasionally inelegant support in O'Linn, described by John Arlott as 'not a technically gifted player; his footwork is at times quite grotesque and often it seems as if he is quite incapable of playing forward at all'. The partnership was progressing and had taken the score to 91 when there occurred a controversial incident – at least it was, but needn't have been if the umpires, Charlie Elliott and Frank Lee, had not been so officious, pig-headed and downright stupid.

O'Linn and McGlew had batted well until within about a quarter of an hour of lunch. They had earned the respect and even the support of the crowd when there occurred the incident which in some ways defined this Test match. Moss was bowling to O'Linn on 45 and O'Linn called McGlew for a quick single. McGlew responded but in going for it collided with Moss accidentally, recovered but had lost so much ground that when Statham threw the ball in and broke the wicket with a direct hit, McGlew was well short. An appeal was made and umpire Charlie Elliott correctly gave McGlew out.

McGlew always accept the umpire's decisions and went. But the less than totally partisan English crowd at Trent Bridge began to disapprove and even a few boos were heard. Cowdrey, nothing if not a fair, honest and decent man, realised that there was something not quite right about this and recalled McGlew. McGlew was unwilling to make a fuss and kept walking, but eventually stopped and began to turn back.

Cowdrey then asked umpires Elliott and Lee if they could have a rethink. The terms he actually used were significant. He apparently asked if they could change their decision, a question to which the answer had to be 'no', for umpire Elliott had made the correct decision, and Cowdrey was effectively asking him to make the wrong decision!

Had Cowdrey actually said 'I am withdrawing my appeal' (as Brian Johnston told the TV viewers at the time that Cowdrey should do) then the answer might have been different. But Cowdrey was clearly seen to indicate to McGlew that there was nothing he could do. McGlew then turned to walk off again, and sympathetic boos reverberated round Trent Bridge.

It was a bizarre and surreal moment. We had both captains in agreement that McGlew should continue his innings. Cowdrey was behaving the way that Englishmen were expected to behave when they felt an injustice was done McGlew was behaving in a way that was more English than the English, as it were, by his reluctance to stay around and argue his case and only came back when the English captain asked him to. But the umpires are totally to blame. They could have shown a little more discretion and sheer common sense, but they decided to be legalistic, unbending and autocratic in inappropriate circumstances when the crowd, a sense of fair play and even the mythical 'spirit of cricket' demanded otherwise. No one was really entirely in the wrong, but cricket was the loser, and another nail was hammered into the coffin of South Africa just at the time when they were showing signs of a comeback. Once again, the non-existent Law 47 should have come into play, namely: 'The umpires shall at all times exercise common sense' … but it didn't.

It was in the afternoon that I saw one of the really sad aspects of Test match cricket when young Colin Wesley managed to pick up what was called a 'king pair', namely being dismissed first ball in each innings. It took me a while to work out what they were talking about. I knew that a duck in each innings was called a 'pair of spectacles' namely a couple of round circles shaped like nothings – I was getting good at working out symbolism! – but a 'king pair' was a new one to me. In Wesley's case his destroyer both times was Brian Statham. Wesley was caught by Subba Row in the first innings and Jim Parks in the second.

I remember being sorry for Colin Wesley, whom by mistake I called Charles Wesley, but that was the man who wrote hymns in the 18th century for the Methodist Church. I love the story (even though it is possibly apocryphal) of how Don Bradman sought him out after his first dismissal to commiserate and to assure Wesley that he (Bradman) had suffered the same fate himself. When it happened the second time, Wesley sought Bradman out and said that he, Bradman, had never suffered a 'king pair'. Bradman smiled and agreed.

But this was Sid O'Linn's finest hour. He continued his resistance, getting some help from Waite for a while and the arrears were wiped off. But before any healthy surplus could be built up, Moss removed the pair of them, trapping Waite lbw with a ball which kept low, and then having O'Linn caught by Cowdrey for 98. It was a shame that he never reached his deserved century but he was given a very impressive standing ovation as he departed. The innings finished soon after that, and England required only 49 to win. The South Africans had scored 247 in their second innings, not in itself a poor total, and an unusual feature had been that there were no extras! Not a wide, nor a no-ball from the bowlers, and a flawless performance from Jim Parks behind the stumps.

Half an hour remained that Saturday night, but there was a very visible determination from Adcock that the Englishmen were not going to get the winning runs on the Saturday. There was always a chance (admittedly slight) that, given this awful summer so far, rain might wipe out play on both Monday and Tuesday. As it was, England reached 25/0 before bad light brought an early close on the Saturday and delayed things until mid-afternoon on the Monday, but England won the Test match and the rubber with a degree of ease.

And thus, the rubber was lost. A great deal of credit has to be given to England who had now for six years in a row won their summer Test series. They had drawn with Pakistan in 1954, and (as the calypso song of the time went) had not lost a series at home since 'these two little friends of mine, Ramadhin and Valentine' had blown that huge hole in the edifice of imperialism and superiority for the West Indies in 1950. The difference was that this year the South Africans had been expected to put up more resistance. The South Africans could claim some sort of excuses in apartheid protesters, the no-ball controversy, the McGlew dismissal and even bad light decisions, but the real reasons for their humiliation lay elsewhere – in their basic inability to play Statham and Trueman. England were simply better.

Third Test Scorecard

ENGLAND FIRST INNINGS

R Subba Row b Tayfield	30
MC Cowdrey c Fellows-Smith b Goddard	67
ER Dexter b Adcock	3
KF Barrington c O'Linn b Goddard	80
MJK Smith lbw b Goddard	0
JM Parks run out	16
R Illingworth c and b Tayfield	37
PM Walker c O'Linn b Tayfield	30
FS Trueman b Goddard	15
JB Statham b Goddard	2
AE Moss not out	3
Extras	4
TOTAL	287

Fall of wickets: 1/57; 2/82; 3/129; 4/129; 5/154; 6/229; 7/241; 8/261; 9/267

Bowling

Adcock	30	2	86	1
Pothecary	20	5	42	0
Fellows-Smith	5	0	17	0
Goddard	42	17	80	5
Tayfield	28.3	11	58	3

SOUTH AFRICA FIRST INNINGS

DJ McGlew c Parks b Trueman	0
TL Goddard run out	16
S O'Linn c Walker b Trueman	1
RA McLean b Statham	11
PR Carlstein c Walker b Statham	2
C Wesley c Subba Row b Statham	0
JP Fellows-Smith not out	31
JHB Waite c Trueman b Moss	1
HJ Tayfield b Trueman	11
JE Pothecary b Trueman	7
NAT Adcock b Trueman	0
Extras	8
TOTAL	88

Fall of wickets: 1/0; 2/12; 3/13; 4/33; 5/33; 6/44; 7/49; 8/68; 9/82

Trueman	14.3	6	27	5
Statham	14	5	27	3
Moss	10	3	26	1

SOUTH AFRICA SECOND INNINGS (following on)

DJ McGlew run out	45
TL Goddard b Trueman	0
JP Fellows-Smith c Illingworth b Trueman	15
RA McLean c Parks b Trueman	0
S O'Linn c Cowdrey b Moss	98
PR Carlstein c Cowdrey b Statham	19
C Wesley c Parks b Statham	0
JHB Waite lbw b Moss	60
HJ Tayfield c Parks b Moss	6
JE Pothecary c Parks b Trueman	3
NAT Adcock not out	1
Extras	0
TOTAL	247

Fall of wickets: 1/1; 2/23; 3/23; 4/91; 5/122; 6/122; 7/231; 8/242; 9/245

Bowling

Trueman	22	3	77	4
Statham	26	3	71	2
Illingworth	19	9	33	0
Moss	15.4	3	36	3
Barrington	3	1	5	0
Dexter	6	2	12	0
Walker	3	0	13	0

ENGLAND SECOND INNINGS

R Subba Row not out	16
MC Cowdrey lbw Goddard	27
ER Dexter c Adcock b Goddard	0
KF Barrington not out	1
Extras	5
TOTAL	49 for 2

Fall of wickets: 1/48; 2/48

Bowling

Adcock	7.4	2	16	0
Pothecary	2	0	15	0
Goddard	5	1	13	2

It might have been thought that the tour was now over, but it still had a couple of months to run! In one sense it was, of course, over but the Springboks now seemed to relax more, some batsmen got runs, and although the rain continued in what was a dreadfully awful summer, some good cricket was played, and in both the remaining Tests South Africa, with the pressure now off them, might even have won. The impression by the end of the tour was that the gap between the two sides wasn't quite as wide as the 3-0 scoreline might have suggested, and one could now look back on the first three Test matches and identify key moments which might well have gone the other way.

The first port of call after the Trent Bridge debacle was still in the Midlands at Leicestershire, certainly not one of the better or more fashionable counties and whose facilities in 1960 were generally regarded as more than a little primitive. Willie Watson, one time of England, was now captain of Leicestershire and he entered into the spirit of things, declaring twice and setting South Africa a reasonable target which they might have reached if it had not been for rain.

Leicestershire's first innings was a massive 287/3 declared. The opening batsmen were Maurice Hallam and a fellow called Harold Bird, who had recently joined the county from his native Yorkshire and who would, in time, be 'Dickie' Bird, the famous umpire. They put on a total of 277 for the first wicket, Leicestershire's highest partnership since before the war. The South Africans' first innings bowling figures were embarrassing, but they fought back with Colin Wesley making amends for his 'king pair' at Trent Bridge by scoring 90 and then in the second innings Goddard took 6-29 before Watson declared, asking the South Africans to make 170 in two hours. McLean and Carlstein looked like getting them for a while, but McLean ran himself out, and the South Africans finished up 12 runs short. It was a shame that so few people were there to see what was a good, if somewhat contrived, game of cricket.

It was the return to Lord's to play Middlesex that saw the South Africans play some of their best cricket for some time. Adcock, who had had a rest when the team were in Leicester, returned to form with length and accuracy, and at last Tayfield found a steady length as Middlesex (with men like Peter Parfitt, John Murray and Fred Titmus on board) were shot out for 191, before the South Africans showed just how well they could bat. Goddard, captaining the side, scored an elegant 142 and was well supported by Pithey, Carlstein and McLean who all hit fifies. The South Africans declared over 200 ahead and an innings victory looked a certainty until a thunderstorm hit the ground on the last morning with Middlesex struggling at 101/4.

This game, however, was upstaged a little in the press by the story and pictures of Geoff Griffin on Monday, 18 July, bowling in the nets at the Nursery End of the ground wearing what the *Daily Mirror* describes as an 'aluminium sheath, 11 inches long, secured by three webbing straps, two below the elbow and one above it'. The purpose of it was to keep the arm rigid and it seemed to be a success as he performed under the scrutiny of his captain Jackie McGlew and Sir Donald Bradman. It had been designed by a 78-year-old New Zealander called Sir Harold Gillies who had used a similar thing to help him play golf.

There was nothing in the laws against it, and it seemed to work well, for Griffin was able to bowl flat out with it on. The prospect was now raised that Griffin might yet, after all, be chosen to play in the fourth Test match beginning later that week at Old Trafford, but in the event nothing more was heard about it. Perhaps the South Africans felt that he might still be no-balled, or perhaps they felt that his confidence had been shot to pieces in any case, but nothing more was heard of this idea.

As for the game v Middlesex itself, the opposition was, of course, different, but it was hard to resist the conclusion that if South Africa had shown the same attitude and determination in even one of those Test matches, things might have been a lot different. The public and the TV audiences felt that they deserved to see a better and more competitive performance from the Springboks in at least one of the remaining Test matches. They got it, to a certain extent at least, when the teams met in Manchester on 21 July.

Or rather they didn't, until Saturday, 23 July. Two days of rain in Manchester reduced the Test to a three-day match, and it is a pity that some of the players, one in particular, did not seem to understand that. One often wonders how Lancashire have been one of the strongest English counties. Certainly, Manchester and Liverpool, and towns like Burnley, Preston, Oldham and Bury are heavily populated centres, children, as it were, of the Industrial Revolution and mad keen on team games like football and cricket with, in the case of cricket, the incentive of their rivalry with Yorkshire – but rain is the curse of the area. Glasgow has a similar problem and that may in part explain why cricket has never taken off there as much as it has in Edinburgh, but certainly

Lancashire, as a general rule, must have more heartbroken and disappointed people on a rainy summer Saturday than anywhere else.

This Test match only started on the Saturday, which gave everyone enough time to discuss the rather strange selections of both teams. South Africa had dropped one of the comparative successes of the last Test in Jonathan Fellows-Smith in preference for the hitherto under-performing Tony Pithey who had, admittedly, reached a half-century against Middlesex but had otherwise done very little of late. England had welcomed back Geoff Pullar from injury and brought in spinner David Allen and batsman Doug Padgett of Yorkshire with Mike Smith, Peter Walker and Alan Moss all dropping out and feeling entitled to wonder 'why me?' Walker was having an argument with the crusty Wilf Wooller of Glamorgan (not difficult to do that!) about the following year's contract, but had shown promise; Moss had been sacrificed so that England could have two spinners – Allen and Illingworth; and Mike Smith, an established batsman was probably being genuinely 'rested', as the series had been won. He would be back.

On a remarkably dry surface, play started on the Saturday, England batting, having won the toss in front of a fair but not huge crowd. England's total was 260 and it could be argued that South Africa had the better of the day with Jim Pothecary picking up his first Test wicket and ending up with 3-85, a useful help to Adcock, who took 4-66. Tayfield might have been expected to do better, but disappointed, with the best bowler, not for the first time on this tour, being Trevor Goddard, who conceded only 26 runs in 24 overs and captured the wickets of Barrington, Parks and Allen.

For England, Barrington top-scored with 76, but the best innings was, not surprisingly, that of Ted Dexter who showed yet again his wide range of strokes. As often happens, however, just as it began to look as if he was beginning to tear the attack part, he missed a straight one from Pothecary and departed for 38. Parks and Illingworth gave Barrington support, but the strength of Ken Barrington was always one of composure, common sense and staying power ('I've booked in for bed and breakfast' was apparently one of his aphorisms) rather than flamboyant stroke play – a quality not always to be despised, and he steered England to a respectable 260 leaving South Africa with a difficult half-hour or so at the end of the Saturday. So far, this game was resembling a three-day county match.

South Africa survived Saturday night, finishing at 17/0 but were soon in trouble on the Monday morning being 92/5 at one point, with McGlew, Goddard, Pithey, Carlstein and Waite all falling to the fast bowling of Statham and Trueman. Another follow-on and an innings defeat were a distinct possibility, but at long last Roy McLean came good and delighted the paltry crowd with a marvellous innings of 109 and showed the Manchester public just how good he was, or, more pertinently, how good he could have been. South African apologists recalled yet again the last day of the first Test match at Edgbaston when an early error by McLean led inexorably to defeat, when it could have been victory.

Today, he was severe on Trueman, Allen, Illingworth and Dexter – on Statham less so – and he found a partner in Sid O'Linn. John Arlott, in a brilliant analogy compares the cavalier McLean to the Spanish hero Don Quixote while O'Linn was the ever-faithful Sancho Panza who supported him, encouraged him and kept up one end of the wicket to let McLean score the runs which eventually brought South Africa up to 229, a respectable reply to England's 260. They were only 31 runs behind, but there was still a day and the best part of two hours to be played. Any result seemed possible, particularly when we had on the field men who were past masters at playing the three-day game, which this Test match had now, in effect, become.

One might have expected Cowdrey to give orders to his batsmen to go for quick runs and set a reasonable declaration, but England were without Subba Row who had broken his thumb while fielding and rather disappointingly were only 50/2 at the close of play, a meagre 81 runs ahead. Even so, it was felt that a result could have been contrived, even if it meant South Africa feeding them runs (which happened in many County Championship games, however much it was denied) or England simply getting a move on to set the Springboks a target. The rubber had been won and lost, and this approach would have given the crowd and television audience something at least to get excited about. As it happened Cowdrey kept going until after tea on the last day as Barrington bored the pants off the Old Trafford crowd, who got more and more restless and then finally began to go home.

England set the South Africans the ridiculous total of 185 in an hour and three-quarters and the game fizzled out with South Africa 46/0 in front of a virtually empty ground. While one can to a certain extent sympathise with Cowdrey in his desire not to lose a game – and no doubt the knives would have been out for him if he had lost – it was hardly an example of Cowdrey or cricket putting their best foot forward in the ongoing attempt to arrest the decline of the game's attraction to spectators. A valid point was surely that the England attack, even without Statham who had tonsillitis, could well have disposed of South Africa for a low score, especially if they had been offered a tempting target. England had already four times that summer dismissed them for less than 200. As it was, the South Africans saw no prospect of winning, and the 'shutters came down' in Brian Johnston's graphic image.

The most important thing was the fans, however, and the disappointment that this brought them. Many people have said that 'football without fans is nothing'. That is hardly true of cricket where many club games are lucky to attract a couple of men and a dog or a courting couple doing their business behind a tree, but nevertheless, it is surely vital to encourage fans to keep going to the professional cricket game. Cricket needed all the supporters that it could get in 1960, and this seemed a rather silly way of antagonising them, especially a holiday crowd at the end of July, not to mention the huge following that television had the potential to attract. It was difficult for me to persuade my jeering friends that cricket was not necessarily always as boring as all this.

For the South Africans, at least it was not a defeat, and they were able to peddle the myth that they might have made a go of it if Cowdrey had been more co-operative. But then again, they themselves lacked the bowling power to dislodge Barrington quickly enough in either innings. Crucially, Barrington seemed able to play Adcock, but he could not beat the Old Trafford public address system. According to John Arlott, his downfall was brought about when the PA announcer gleefully told the now somnolent Lancashire crowd that Lancashire had beaten Surrey at

The Oval. This was, of course, bad news for Surrey's Ken Barrington who promptly lost concentration and cut a ball from Goddard, which he would have been better to leave alone, into the hands of Waite!

Fourth Test Scorecard

ENGLAND FIRST INNINGS

G Pullar b Pothecary	12
R Subba Row lbw b Adcock	27
ER Dexter b Pothecary	38
MC Cowdrey c Waite b Adcock	20
KF Barrington b Goddard	76
DEV Padgett c Wesley b Pothecary	5
JM Parks lbw b Goddard	36
R Illingworth not out	22
DA Allen lbw b Goddard	0
FS Trueman c Tayfield b Adcock	10
JB Statham b Adcock	0
Extras	14
TOTAL	260

Fall of wickets: 1/27; 2/85; 3/108; 4/113; 5/134; 6/197; 7/239; 8/239; 9/260

Bowling

Adcock	23	5	66	4
Pothecary	28	3	85	3
Goddard	24	16	26	3
Tayfield	18	3	69	0

SOUTH AFRICA FIRST INNINGS

DJ McGlew c Subba Row b Trueman	32
TL Goddard c Parks b Statham	8
AJ Pithey c Parks b Statham	7
PR Carlstein b Trueman	11
RA McLean b Allen	109
JHB Waite b Statham	11
S O'Linn c sub b Allen	27
C Wesley c Trueman b Allen	3
HJ Tayfield c Trueman b Allen	4
JE Pothecary b Trueman	12
NAT Adcock not out	0
Extras	5
TOTAL	229

Fall of wickets: 1/25; 2/33; 3/57; 4/62; 5/92; 6/194; 7/198; 8/202; 9/225

Bowling

Statham	22	11	32	3
Trueman	20	2	58	3
Dexter	17	5	41	0
Allen	19.5	6	58	4
Illingworth	11	2	35	0

ENGLAND SECOND INNINGS

G Pullar c and b Pothecary	9
MC Cowdrey b Adcock	25
ER Dexter c McLean b Pothecary	22
KF Barrington c Waite b Goddard	35
DEV Padgett c Waite b Adcock	2
JM Parks c and b Goddard	20
R Illingworth c McLean b Adcock	5
DA Allen not out	14
FS Trueman not out	14
Extras	7
TOTAL	153/7 declared

Fall of wickets: 1/23; 2/41; 3/63; 4/65; 5/71; 6/101; 7/134

Bowling

Adcock	27	9	59	3
Pothecary	32	10	61	2
Goddard	16	5	26	2

SOUTH AFRICA SECOND INNINGS

DJ McGlew not out	26
TL Goddard not out	16
Extras	4
TOTAL	46/0

Bowling

Trueman	6	1	10	0
Statham	4	2	3	0
Allen	7	4	5	0
Illingworth	5	3	6	0
Pullar	1	0	6	0
Padgett	2	0	8	0
Cowdrey	1	0	4	0

It was now down to The Oval to meet Surrey at the end of July. Surrey had been County Champions (deservedly) from 1952 to 1958, seven years in a row, and although they were now in a slight decline, they were still one of the better counties, with Micky Stewart, John Edrich, Roy Swetman, Tony Lock and the Bedser twins. Before the game, Lock was seen to be in earnest discussion with Geoff Griffin, no doubt about the villainies of umpires who called bowlers for no-balls! Tony had himself been the victim of a few no-ball calls. Interestingly, the press did not seem to turn hysterical about this, nor did Gubby Allen get hot under the collar about Tony Lock. One gets the uncomfortable feeling that, had Lock been a South African, Australian or even a Yorkshireman, it might have been a different story.

The Surrey match was another occasion, not unlike the recent Test match, when a reasonable effort might have been made to make a game of it, but things were allowed to drift into the tamest of draws, to the disappointment of the crowd. The South Africans made 338/6 declared with John Waite hitting a slow 125, then Surrey saved the follow-on and declared their first innings at lunchtime when they were still 115 behind. The South Africans took their time about putting on another 67 runs before their declaration, while Surrey then batted out the last afternoon in a singularly pointless game of cricket. Once again, the 'brighter cricket' lobby had grist for their mill, as supporters began to yawn and yearn for the now imminent football season. Clearly Jackie McGlew had had his fingers burnt by the game at Northants at the end of

May, but *Wisden* reports acidly, 'There was not much in the play of either side to attract support.'

CHAPTER 8

AUGUST

THERE WERE three weeks and therefore six cricket matches scheduled between the fourth and fifth Test matches. In the event, only five games were played, for the game against Sussex between 10-12 August was wiped out without a ball being bowled. It was nevertheless a busy schedule, punctuated by the usual concomitant of 1960, and indeed most English cricket seasons – the bad weather.

Inevitably now the tour began to fade from public attention. The rubber was dead but there was also a new football season beginning to appear, and this year there was an additional sporting attraction in the shape of the Olympic Games due to start in the Eternal City of Rome at the end of August. Trials were being held for selection in various events and featured on television. It was not that Britain were likely to do well, however. In the end, they won two gold medals – Anita Lonsbrough in the women's 200-metres breaststroke and Don Thompson in the men's 50-kilometre walk. It would be South Africa's last participation in the Olympic Games under their old system. Already there were a few mutterings about them, with the African nations showing clear signs of being less tolerant than the world of cricket was.

It was the first time that the Olympics had been brought to the people of Great Britain by television in any meaningful way. In 1948 they had been in London, but very few people had a television then. The same was true, to a lesser extent, of the Olympics in Helsinki in 1952, and Melbourne in 1956 was simply too far away for live television and in the middle of the night in any case. Film coverage arrived about three days later, although by 1958/59 the Ashes series was shown slightly quicker than that – usually about the same time as the next day's play was beginning, with all sorts of unlikely stories about pictures being bounced off satellites in Singapore and other barely comprehensible stuff. Such was the brave new world of the television age.

But Rome in 1960 was a good target for the much-vaunted Eurovision (already the host to an impressive song contest!) and the swimming and athletics in particular were well enjoyed, the highlight being the evening of Saturday, 27 August when it was difficult to say which was the more impressive – Anita Lonsbrough's gold-medal swim or David Coleman's lung-bursting commentary on the event! It was a great night for the unpretentious Yorkshire girl, and indeed for all British swimming supporters, because gold medals didn't come round very often in those days. Six had been won by British competitors in 1956; two was a distinct disappointment in 1960.

For all sorts of reasons then, cricket began to disappear from public consciousness. From time to time, the press brought up the Griffin affair again and tried to get him selected for the fifth Test match at The Oval, but his bowling days were over, at least as far as this tour was concerned.

Demonstrations kept happening against apartheid, sometimes outside hotels where the Springboks were staying, sometimes outside the grounds where they were playing, but it was all very sporadic, and there was nothing that one could honestly describe as a concerted campaign. In these circumstances, the protesters didn't really manage to attract the media attention that they would have liked. Their demonstrations were far too polite, and journalistic discussions on apartheid were in severe danger of becoming a national bore; left-wing journals usually ending up by saying something along the lines of 'South Africa must address this problem very soon' and the right-wing newspapers said that apartheid wasn't all that bad, and that we should 'allow South Africa to solve its own problems'.

August began with the South Africans in Wales again, this time at Swansea and for the second time they beat Glamorgan. It was a rain-affected game, but conditions suited Hugh Tayfield, who took 7-51 in the first innings and 5-90 in the second. On the other hand, the South African batting in the first innings would have to be described as poor as they collapsed for 151 to that old Glamorgan warhorse Don Shepherd, whose figures of 8-45 were one of his career highlights. By the time that the South Africans came to bat in the second innings, conditions had dried out, and requiring 130 in two hours, they achieved that target with the loss of only one wicket. Jackie McGlew had an outstanding knock of 76 not out.

There followed a somewhat pedestrian game at Edgbaston on 3-5 August, where Warwickshire declined to accept South Africa's none-too-generous victory target of 281 in three hours and the game fizzled out into a tame draw. Highlights for the tourists were some fine batting from Sid O'Linn – 61 and 150 not out – and another good performance with the ball from Hugh Tayfield, who took 6-66 in the first innings.

And now to Yorkshire! This game at Bramall Lane would normally have been one of the highlights of the tour, with spice added to it by the fact that Yorkshire, traditionally, tended to do badly against the South Africans. As it happened, Trueman was dropped or rested, the better to preserve him for Yorkshire's push for the County Championship, and the game was poorly attended at that grand old stadium which was clearly showing its age and was by then more associated with Sheffield United FC in public perception than the scene of many an epic Test match of bygone days. The word 'dour' is often applied to Yorkshiremen, both in their social demeanour and in their batting, and there was a distinct lack of stroke play about Yorkshire's miserable total of 198, a total, however, which began to look good when Illingworth spun South Africa out for 103.

The Springbok cause was not helped when Tony Pithey took ill and had to retire from the game, but after that the middle order of Wesley, McLean, Carlstein and O'Linn were all out for single figures. Then, unaccountably, when the South Africans were offered the victory target of 236 in two sessions, they refused to take it. This target, unlike some others which had been set during that summer, was by no means beyond them, but the Springboks finished the game at 91/4 to the sound of boos and slow handclapping from the small and angry Yorkshire crowd which had paid good 'brass' to get in to watch all this. Although the South Africans were a batsman short, Yorkshire's attack was also depleted without Trueman, and the crowd felt that the tourists might at least have given them some entertainment. It was not one of the better days of the tour.

The tour was now in every sense losing momentum and steam. After Sheffield, it was down to Hove to play Sussex – or rather it would have been if it had not rained continuously for three days, a rare but not unprecedented happening on the south coast in August. But the hospitality of the Sussex fellows was second to none, and it was almost as if it were a holiday, with one or two of the tourists not above admitting to the press that they were far from displeased at this turn of events.

They were rested, and it was no coincidence that the next two games were possibly their best of the tour with a fine win over a strong Kent side at Canterbury, and then the final Test at The Oval, which, but for the rain on the last day, they might well have won.

The game at Canterbury indicated, not for the first time on the tour, that spin was the strong point of South Africa's attack, with Atholl McKinnon doing enough to earn a place in the Oval Test match with 7-73 and 4-62 as Kent were defeated by 160 runs after being bowled out for 192 and 155. Another pleasing aspect of this game was

Jonathan Fellows-Smith hitting a half-century in each innings and making one wonder why his Test selection had been in doubt earlier in the summer.

And so to The Oval for the fifth Test match beginning on 18 August. England gave a cap to Tommy Greenhough of Lancashire, the unusual thing about him being that he was a leg-spinner. He was chosen in place of Illingworth who had not had a great game at Old Trafford, but also often gave the impression that his 'face didn't fit' with England. Certainly, later events (in Australia in 1970/71) would bear out the contention that there was never a strong relationship between himself and Colin Cowdrey. South Africa also, at last, brought in a spinner, Atholl McKinnon at the expense of Tony Pithey.

Cowdrey yet again won the toss and made the decision to bat first. It did not seem to be a clear-cut decision, for the weather was unpredictable, with a total of six showers during the first day. It was a good day for South Africa. Adcock put in a strong performance, as did the fast-improving Tony Pothecary, and early on the Friday England were back in the pavilion for 155, Adcock having taken 6-65 and Pothecary 4-58. For

England, only Geoff Pullar with 59 put on any kind of a score.

The ball was now very definitely, possibly for the first time that summer, in South Africa's court, and they did indeed finish the Friday 12 runs ahead and with seven wickets left, but the way they went about their business left a little to be desired. Whether they had decided to be ultra cautious or whether they simply lacked the ability to take a grip of the game, no one can really tell, but once again the crowd (and it was a larger one than usual on this day) felt themselves short-changed by the lack of action and even by the South Africans appealing successfully against the light when they were well on top. It made no sense at all. Most wise captains only use the light as a weapon when they are doing badly or are vulnerable. When they are doing well, it is important to keep the momentum going.

There is often a feeling that creeps into a team after repeated beatings that they are somehow not 'allowed' or not 'destined' to win. This certainly happens in football, and cricket too. This was a prime example. South Africa were well on top but refused to go for the jugular. It was a mistake that the Australians in the 1990s, for example, never made. They got on top and stayed on top. There was no 'death wish' about them, but here South Africa, in the unaccustomed position of being on top, allowed the initiative to slip.

The tedium continued on Saturday and South Africa were eventually bowled out for 419, giving them a more than comfortable lead of 264. In some ways it was a triumph for the Springboks, and they had every reason to be confident of victory, in spite of their earlier failure to grasp the game. There had been one unfortunate incident of the type that this tour already had plenty of. Goddard had batted painstakingly and conscientiously to reach 99 when he edged one to Cowdrey in the slips. Cowdrey, with a reputation of always being fair and honest, wasn't sure whether he had caught it cleanly or not, and umpire Eddie Phillipson shared his doubts. However, the other umpire Charlie Elliott had a clear view, nodded to Phillipson, and Goddard departed one short of what would have been his maiden 100.

It was sad for Goddard, but such decisions are always difficult, and Cowdrey behaved honourably. The crowd were sympathetic to Goddard, but unlike previous happenings on the tour, there was no criticism of anyone. Goddard's reception as he walked back was possibly what he would remember most of a tour in which, it has to be said, he did not always enjoy the best of luck. To his credit, there was a distinct lack of whinging about the decision (which was probably the correct one), a dignified silence being the order of the day, although Goddard, apparently, himself suspected privately that the decision was the wrong one and that Cowdrey knew that he had not caught the ball cleanly. But then again, getting out on 99 is always a painful experience.

Sunday was spent with the South Africans generally quite pleased with themselves and anticipating a victory. Losing a Test series 1-3 was a lot better than losing it 0-3, and they must have felt confident that they could do it. After all, 264 runs were an awful lot to play with, and given good weather there seemed to be nothing to stop them. Certainly, their supporters back home were becoming animated about the possibility.

But then things changed on the Monday. The weather was a little dodgy, but more or less a full day's play was possible, and England's openers Pullar and Cowdrey put on a gigantic 290 for the first wicket, effectively wiping out the arrears and putting England well in credit at 380/4 at the close of play. The batting was good, with the left-handed Pullar the butt of repeated weak jokes from Brian Johnston that he was a good 'puller' (which were funny the first time you heard them), and Cowdrey was simply majestic, showing what a great batsman he was. It was not that the South Africans bowled badly – it was simply that they were not good enough to get the better of the two England openers at their best. By lunchtime the body language of the South Africans in the field indicated that depression and the all-too-prevalent death-wish was beginning to get the better of them once again.

The key moment came when England were 14/0 and Cowdrey was on 8. 'Spud' Pothecary, beginning to impress press, pundits and public more and more, bowled an outswinger to Cowdrey who could not resist a nibble and edged a reasonably simple catch to McLean at second slip. It was fast, but not difficult. Sadly for McLean, who had had quite a few unfortunate moments during the summer, the ball went in and out again, and although one can never say that this was the moment a Test match was lost or drawn, it was certainly significant. Cowdrey then proceeded to pile on another 147 runs before he unaccountably shouldered arms to Goddard and was palpably lbw. Pullar continued, to reach 175, and close of play saw England 116 ahead with six wickets left and the match poised in a fascinating position with all results possible. Significantly there had been a few signs that the pitch was slowly becoming receptive to spin.

And yet again we have to come to the conclusion that the real problem for South Africa was the lack of anyone to partner Adcock. Pothecary was definitely improving but Griffin would have made a difference if he had been allowed to bowl. Once again, one is at a loss to understand why Peter Heine or someone else was not brought in to join the squad. Pothecary's 0-93 and Adcock's 1-106 in the second innings really spoke for themselves. The spinners had slightly more success, but Tayfield in particular was expensive.

The game never really sparkled on Tuesday. England plodded along, putting on another 100 in the morning session, when really the big guns should have been blazing. The conditions were by no means ideal but that does not excuse the lack of imagination, and wickets began to fall. Nine wickets were down by the time that Cowdrey declared at lunch, setting South Africa 216 to get in three hours.

This was by no means an unachievable target, and it would have been a good game, one feels, if the weather had co-operated. But it didn't, and the loss of half an hour to rain in the middle of the afternoon effectively put an end to the game, with South Africa finishing at 97/4. The press were quite right to criticise both teams for not making more of a spectacle of it, for although, at the end of the day, there is not very much one can do when heavy rain comes on, nevertheless, the game could have been over and done with one way or another before it reached that stage. Both sides were guilty of batting too slowly and cautiously at times when they didn't really need to. In particular, Friday night and Saturday morning were times when the South Africans really should have piled on the runs a lot more quickly against a demoralised England attack, then declared a great deal earlier than they did. As it was, McGlew's decision to let things sag was a fatal mistake.

The rubber was, after all, dead. England had won. Surprisingly in these circumstances a large crowd had turned up, even on the last day, and they really deserved to see better. Those who make pious statements about 'spectators must not be allowed to influence the game' do so at their peril. More and more in 1960, spectators were beginning to make it known that they were not to be trifled with. In a few years' time the game would begin to evolve to one-day cricket. This idea horrified purists, but the purists had to answer the question about why the game, as it stood, was not more entertaining. Games in 1960 like the fourth Test match, the fifth Test match and several Springbok games against the counties, had not really done enough to entertain the public. Cricket was failing to realise that it had to move with the times.

Cricket no longer had a captive audience whom it could take for granted. Television again played a big part in all this, for 'the box' brought more and more sports into people's living rooms. Even leaving aside the Olympics, amateur boxing, rowing, snooker, greyhound racing, rugby league, badminton, athletics (indoor in the winter), ice dancing and even wrestling were beginning to appear as well, and sports fans began to develop an interest in sports that they had not hitherto had much acquaintance with. Cricket would, therefore, really have to fight for its survival. It could ill afford to alienate or bore people in the way that the fifth Test match in particular certainly did.

Fifth Test Scorecard

ENGLAND FIRST INNINGS

G Pullar c Goddard b Pothecary	59
MC Cowdrey b Adcock	11
ER Dexter b Adcock	28
KF Barrington lbw b Pothecary	1
MJK Smith b Adcock	0
DEV Padgett c Waite b Pothecary	13
JM Parks c Waite b Pothecary	23
DA Allen lbw b Adcock	0
FS Trueman lbw b Adcock	0
JB Statham not out	13
T Greenhough b Adcock	2
Extras	5
TOTAL	155

Fall of wickets: 1/27; 2/89; 3/91; 4/96; 5/107; 6/125; 7/130; 8/130; 9/142

Bowling

Adcock	31.3	10	65	6
Pothecary	29	9	58	4
Goddard	14	6	25	0
McKinnon	2	1	2	0

SOUTH AFRICA FIRST INNINGS

DJ McGlew c Smith b Greenhough	22
TL Goddard c Cowdrey b Statham	99
JP Fellows-Smith c Smith b Dexter	35
RA McLean lbw b Dexter	0
JHB Waite c Trueman b Dexter	77
S O'Linn b Trueman	55
PR Carlstein b Greenhough	42
JE Pothecary run out	4
HJ Tayfield not out	46
AH McKinnon run out	22
NAT Adcock b Trueman	1
Extras	16
TOTAL	419

Fall of wickets: 1/44; 2/107; 3/107; 4/222; 5/252; 6/326; 7/330; 8/374; 9/412

Bowling

Trueman	31.1	4	93	2
Statham	38	8	96	1
Dexter	30	5	79	3
Greenhough	44	17	99	2
Allen	28	15	36	0

ENGLAND SECOND INNINGS

G Pullar st Waite b McKinnon	175
MC Cowdrey lbw b Goddard	155
ER Dexter b Tayfield	16
KF Barrington c Carlstein b McKinnon	10
MJK Smith c Goddard b Tayfield	11
DEV Padgett run out	31
JM Parks c Waite b Adcock	17
DA Allen not out	12
FS Trueman b Goddard	24
JB Statham c Pothecary b Goddard	4
Extras	24
TOTAL	479/9 declared

Fall of wickets: 1/290; 2/339; 3/362; 4/373; 5/387; 6/412; 7/447; 8/475; 9/479

Bowling

Adcock	38	8	106	1
Pothecary	27	5	93	0
Goddard	27	6	69	3
Tayfield	37	14	108	2
McKinnon	24	7	62	2
Fellows-Smith	4	0	17	0

SOUTH AFRICA SECOND INNINGS

DJ McGlew c Allen b Statham	16
TL Goddard c Cowdrey b Statham	28
JP Fellows-Smith c Parks b Trueman	6
PR Carlstein lbw Trueman	13
RA McLean not out	32
JHB Waite not out	1
Extras	1
TOTAL	97/4

Fall of wickets: 1/21; 2/30; 3/52; 4/89

Bowling

Trueman	10	0	34	2
Statham	12	1	57	2
Allen	2	1	2	0
Greenhough	5.	2	3	0
Dexter	0.2	0	0	0

So, the South Africans lost the Test series 0-3. They had little cause for complaint. But the tour was not yet over. The Combined Services, AER Gilligan's XI, a Lancashire XI (not really the official Lancashire team) and TN

Pearce's XI awaited. The names tell us a great deal about the times, and the differences between 1960 and 2021.

The Combined Services were a mixture of the Army, the Royal Navy and the Royal Air Force. They were a potent team, for the country still had something called National Service. It would stop altogether in 1961 and was already on its way out in 1960, but it meant basically that every young man had to serve two years in one of the three services, whether he wanted to or not. It became a sort of national game trying to avoid this dreadful invasion of one's privacy, which played havoc with lives, romances and careers. All sorts of rubbish involving words like 'duty' and 'service' was thrown about, but it impressed fewer and fewer people, particularly the young, who suddenly developed 'sore backs', 'flat feet' and 'ingrowing toenails' to dodge the column. Those in favour of National Service argued that it allowed young men to 'see the world', 'to learn a little discipline' and to wear a uniform, which apparently could be guaranteed to inflame the sexual desires of young women. Those who were against it, however, were increasingly in the majority, and the services themselves were less and less keen on the idea of dealing with reluctant conscripts in an age of peace.

National Service meant, however, that the Combined Services were a reasonably good cricket team in 1960, but the game at Portsmouth on 27-30 August attracted little attention as the Rome Olympics had now started. Both Great Britain and South Africa were competing there: neither of them doing very well, it has to be said. The opposition to South Africa, although steadily gaining ground, had not yet reached the stage of banning them. And yet one has to wonder how it was that the South Africans did not themselves wonder at the phenomenal success of black athletes from the United States. Wilma Rudolph, for example, 'the Black Gazelle', won three gold medals in Rome. It did not seem to give any backing to the outrageous nonsense about 'racial inferiority' of black people. Pennies had not yet dropped in South Africa about that one.

Against the Combined Services, the South Africans did not bat particularly well in their first innings to reach 239, although Colin Wesley entertained the crowd for a spell with a good 64. The bowling of the 'soldiers and sailors' was good enough, but that could not be said about their batting, for they were dismissed for 103 and 110, having no answer to Tayfield in the first innings and Adcock in the second. In between the Combined Services innings, Goddard hit his fourth century of the tour. It was a competent South African victory.

While this game was going on, the County Championship was resolved in favour of Yorkshire, who beat Worcestershire at Harrogate. It was their 17th win out of 32 games in the championship and full credit was due to Vic Wilson, the professional captain. It was Trueman with his 132 wickets for an average of 12.79 who was the main thrust of their charge to win the title for the second year in a row, but there were also fine batting performances from Doug Padgett, Brian Close and Bryan Stott who all hit well in excess of 1,000 runs for the county. The balance of power had now definitely swung northwards from Surrey to Yorkshire. Lancashire were the runners-up.

And then for the South Africans it was down to Hastings to play AER Gilligan's XI. Arthur Gilligan was an interesting character who had led England to victory in the 1924 series v South Africa, after he had played there with England in 1922/23. He had been a great bowler for Sussex and England, and also been captain of England in 1924/25 in Australia. Less respectably, and ironically in view of who the opposition were today, he had had connections with the British Fascist movement in the mid-1920s. It is possibly easy to make too much of this, because in the 1920s the Fascist movement was nothing like as sinister as it would become, being based on the apparent success of Mussolini's Italy in the 1920s, and before Il Duce 'the jackal' became the lapdog of the Führer. There is no evidence that Gilligan kept up his connection for long, and certainly he was no apologist for Hitler.

Gilligan was a charming host in this slightly anachronistic fixture, and the cricket was good, South Africa winning by 113 runs. Gilligan's XI contained men like Rohan Kanhai, Tony Lock and Peter Loader, but South Africa batted well, Colin Wesley and Tony Pithey (both of whom had had disappointing tours) hitting half-centuries in the first innings and Roy McLean scoring a century in the second. It was McLean's hitting, backed up by that of Jim Pothecary, which allowed McGlew to set a target of 292, which was too much for Gilligan's men.

It was from one seaside town to another for the penultimate game, and that was to Blackpool to play a team whom some called Lancashire, but others, possibly more accurately, would call 'A Lancashire XI', for there were a few youngsters and guests on show. Blackpool was, of course, in its heyday in 1960 the epicentre of British holiday-making. It would not last long this way, for within a few years creeping affluence and prosperity would allow the British working class to contemplate going to Spain for a package holiday, and Blackpool would lose a great deal of its attraction. There was enough evidence on day one of the match to show why Spain was preferable, because torrential rain wiped out any possibility of a full day's play.

It also wiped out any chance of a large crowd, but it did mean the pitch was drying and wickets fell quickly as the Lancashire team were dismissed for 90, 52 of which came from the bat of left-handed veteran and chronic under-performer Alan Wharton. Geoff Griffin opened the batting for the South Africans but was bowled by Ken Higgs for 2 as the Springboks made 198, probably in the context of the game, a reasonable total. Goddard took 5-60 as the Lancastrians scored 173 in the second innings, leaving South Africa 66 to win, which they managed, after a few scares, for the loss of five wickets.

And this eventful, interesting, significant but ultimately disappointing tour finally came to an end at yet another seaside town of Scarborough. The game was against TN Pearce's XI. Tom Pearce had been captain of Essex before the Second World War and on retirement became an England selector. He was often given the job of picking a team for the last match of the season at the Scarborough Festival against the tourists. The weather was predictably glorious and everyone usually wondered why the season was coming to an end in such fine and conducive conditions.

This year was no exception and saw a very competitive game with Trueman, Dexter, Barrington, Tom Graveney and Smith all playing for the TN Pearce's side. South Africa won by four wickets, the highlights being 82 from Peter Carlstein and the left-arm spin of Colin Wesley, both young men giving examples of what might have been for them on the tour. The tour was completed by the band playing the Scottish Jacobite anthem 'Will Ye No' Come Back Again?' and then (contradictorily, perhaps) the Hanoverian 'God Save the Queen'.

CHAPTER NINE

REFLECTIONS

THE 1960 South African tour will not go down as one of English cricket's great summers. It was, however, a very significant one in the history of cricket, in some ways a watershed leading to a few questions beginning to be asked about cricket and society in general. It would be nice to add that summer 1960 also marked a turning point in South Africa's internal political system and the way that it saw itself vis-à-vis the rest of the world. Sadly, that was not the case, although it remains a mystery why no one really asked questions about the system. Macmillan's 'Wind of Change' speech, Sharpeville and the admittedly muted protests in Great Britain should have led someone at least to wonder about such things. It turned out to be apartheid South Africa's second-last tour of the UK, because they had a half-tour in late 1965 in which they played some wonderful cricket, and then the 1970 tour had to be cancelled more or less at the last minute because of fear of demonstrations and disorder. Any slight sympathy for South Africa had long gone, however. South Africa had themselves cancelled the 1968/69 tour of England to South Africa, because England had included Basil D'Oliveira, who was actually a South African and what was called a 'Cape coloured'. He had played several times for England and indeed played a not insignificant role in the Ashes series of 1968.

This was a piece of preposterous arrogance on the part of the South African government, who seemed to think that they were entitled to have a say in who was going to play for the opposition! Frankly, it defied belief! Even the ultra-conservatives in Great Britain who had told us all along that South Africa was not as bad as it was painted, could hardly defend this high-handed diktat. The MCC and the 'keep politics out of sport' lobby were silenced.

There was a curious chiasmus, incidentally, in 1968. The political right told us how bad the Soviet Union was and that South Africa could do with a few minor reforms but was basically all right. The left said the exact opposite. Sadly in 1968 both the Soviet Union and South Africa proved their detractors correct, when the South Africans tried to choose England's cricket team, and the Soviet Union invaded Czechoslovakia! The Soviet Union and South Africa had a great deal in common, mainly an astonishing arrogance towards the rest of the world, a distinct reluctance to move towards the position of everyone else, and a tragic inability to handle those who disagreed with them.

Before 1968, England had played in South Africa in the winter of 1964/65 and had won 1-0, but summer 1965 showed the English public the better and more acceptable side of South African cricket. It was only a half-tour in the second half of the season, the first half of the season having seen a weak New Zealand team lose 0-3. This may have lulled England into a false sense of security for the South Africans were a different matter altogether and probably deserved to win with a far bigger margin than

1-0. Features of the side were the performances of the Pollock brothers and the brilliant cover-point fielding of Colin Bland. It was fine cricket, and it is sad to think that the South Africans were not to come back to England until 1994.

By the late 1960s and 1970, things had moved on with a distinct and visible mood change about apartheid. The protests in Great Britain were more visible and noisy, and with a Labour government now in power, the protesters were not dismissed as freaks and drop-outs quite so much as they had been in 1960. Indeed it was only the lunatic fringe on the right (often expatriates who had themselves come from Rhodesia and South Africa) who were prepared to make any kind of defence of the system. There were also, perhaps, a few of the South African players themselves who were beginning to wonder. After all, the question of whether South Africa was out of step with the rest of the world or the other way round really did answer itself, did it not?

Sadly, the 1960 tour of England did not change much in South Africa. One would have hoped that some of the South African tourists who had been on the same field in England as Rohan Kanhai, for example, and Ron Headley, would have at least posed the question why this could not happen in their own land? But, sadly, they didn't, so much in tune were they to the way that they had been brought up. John Waite's book *Perchance to Bowl*, an excellent account of the cricketing side of the tour, also contains sad examples of Waite's political views. One would like to think that some of it was written tongue in cheek. One would also like to think that Waite's extreme and sometimes ridiculous views were idiosyncratic and not shared by his team-mates. Sadly, neither of these contentions seems to have been the case.

And yet, in the early 1960s in Great Britain and elsewhere, young people were beginning to at least question the morals and values of their society. Institutions like the church, the royal family and the armed forces began to feel themselves under threat, as pop music and affluence began to take a grip of society. This can be paralleled in the USA and in Europe. It did not seem to happen in South Africa, until it was far too late.

There was of course an increasing 'problem' (if one wanted to define it in such terms – many people saw it as an 'opportunity') with race in Great Britain. Since the late 1940s, Commonwealth citizens had arrived in Great Britain in search of a better life. Whether they found it is open to question, but only a fool would deny that they faced a great deal of prejudice. It wasn't always in the naked, brick-throwing aggression of the ignorant; more often it lay in the 'I have nothing against them but...' attitude of the middle classes and the aspirant working classes, who all dreaded the thought that a family of 'them' might come and live next door, or worse still, that one of 'them' might entertain romantic desires for one of the daughters of the house.

This would be a problem for many years in Britain, the hatred of the immigrants being polarised by a despicable character called Enoch Powell, who managed to make such prejudice respectable. But even the Conservative Party found him to be a bit much, and duly dissociated itself from his outbursts. Incredibly, Powell had once been professor of Greek at the University of Sydney in Australia, and was generally reckoned to be an expert on the very cosmopolitan Herodotus. One would have thought that this might have rubbed off on him. But Powell was more like the violent Athenian demagogue Cleon: a very potent rabble-rouser. Sadly he was also 'deinos legein' – the Greek phrase literally meaning 'terrible at speaking' but which means 'terribly good at speaking,' i.e. a serious menace and threat because of his excellent oratory. Powell influenced many people who really should have known a great deal better. It would have been better if he had been a less inspirational speaker.

Only a few weeks after the Springboks returned home, there was a major political event in South Africa. This was a referendum, on 5 October 1960, in which South Africa voted to become a republic. When we say 'South Africa voted', we mean of course that the white South Africans voted. The vote itself highlighted a further division within South Africa, for the vote against the British monarchy was particularly strong in the former Boer republics of Transvaal and the Orange Free State.

This was only to be expected. The Boer republics were still smarting from their defeat in the war of 60 years ago, and they certainly resented what they saw as interference from the British Commonwealth countries and from Harold Macmillan's 'Wind of Change'. They had no reason to love the British royal family. Clearly South African politics was far more complex than anyone realised and indeed was difficult to follow from the viewpoint of Great Britain two continents away.

Yet it does seem difficult to understand why men with good English and Scottish names like McGlew, McLean, Adcock, Fellows-Smith and McKinnon did not at this point say, 'Wait a minute!' Why could the 'British' provinces not have said, 'No! We want to stay part of the British Commonwealth, we want to continue to play cricket, we are prepared to loosen apartheid with a view to its total abolition in ten years, we want to see a multi-racial South African cricket team play against the West Indies and India and Pakistan.' It would have saved a great many problems if they had done that, but instead they opted to stay under Verwoerd, Vorster and the Boers. They might have earned the admiration and gratitude of the world for emancipating the blacks in the same way as Winston Churchill and Montgomery had freed Europe from slavery. Instead, astonishingly, they chose to identify with the Boers and their evil quasi-Nazi views of racial superiority.

This is a shame. Cricket itself would suffer for the next 30 years or so from South Africa and its repercussions, but more immediately, the throwing controversy did not exactly die down, although it became a great deal less prominent. Ian Meckiff was not chosen for the 1961 Australian tour of England, and those who felt that the hounding of Geoff Griffin was all about preventing the England batsmen from having to face Ian Meckiff, were proud of themselves. But the 1961 season was as good as the 1960 season had been bad, with Richie Benaud's Australians winning the hearts of the British public by some fine performances as the Englishmen contributed to their own fate with a few spectacular pieces of self-destruction.

But before that happened, and just at the time when the world of cricket needed such a boost, there came a wonderful series between Australia, led by Richie Benaud, and the West Indies, led by Frank Worrell. There was still an element of colour consciousness in Australia at this point, for Australia had pursued its notorious 'White Australia' policy as regards immigration, but this policy was weakening and the West Indians drove a horse and cart through it with their wonderful play and general demeanour in a marvellously competitive and always enjoyable Test match series.

Australia won 2-1, but the most famous Test matches were the two that did not produce a definite winner. The first Test in Brisbane was the famous first-ever 'tied Test match' of 737 runs each, and the fourth Test in Adelaide saw Australia's last two, Ken MacKay and Lindsay Kline, defy the West Indies when all seemed lost. At the end the West Indians were given a tremendous send-off from a grateful nation who had enjoyed a magnificent series of cricket. Once again, one has to wonder how this astounding success (in every respect) went down in South Africa.

As far as England were concerned, there can be little doubt that 1960 hastened changes in the game. Too many games were simply boring, and limited-overs cricket soon began to make an appearance, the first 65-overs-per-side tournament being introduced in 1963. It was a success, won by Sussex, and by 1969 there was a 40-overs-per-side televised game on BBC2 every Sunday in a special Sunday League. Things change very slowly in cricket, but when they do change, they change radically. Another limited-overs competition appeared in the early 1970s, and sadly the next change was the Packer Circus of the late 1970s, something that was, frankly and deplorably, driven by little other than sheer greed.

As for myself, the summer of 1960 had a profound effect. My love of cricket was confirmed, and it had a very important indirect side-effect. I had started secondary school on the Monday of the fifth Test match. I was put in the top class, the one that was allowed to learn Latin. I knew nothing about this subject, but my love of cricket encouraged me to read loads of 'school' books like the Billy Bunter series by Frank Richards, and the Jennings books of Anthony Buckeridge. The boys in these schools seemed to do little else other than play cricket and, in the classroom, they studied Latin under a grim character called Quelch in the case of Bunter and Wilkins in the case of Jennings. So, modelling myself on and identifying with Harry Wharton and Bob Cherry, I decided that I would be good at Latin – and of course, in education, there is such a thing as the self-fulfilling prophecy. If you decide to do something and stick to it, nothing will stop you!

It was from my study of Classics as well that I became, eventually, able to understand – but never to justify – apartheid. The Greeks and the Romans were after all Imperial creatures, something that perhaps explains the popularity of their languages in Victorian Britain, and the success of their empires depended on slavery and their ability to keep everyone else in subjection. Aeneas for example is told in Book VI of the *Aeneid in the Underworld* that although others, the Greeks presumably, can be good at art and sculpting, it was the duty of the Romans to '*debellare superbos*' and to '*parcere subiectis*' – to defeat the proud but to spare those who had surrendered.

Pax Romana very soon became Pax Britannica, and 'those who had surrendered' were not to be massacred (although there were more than a few of such lamentable occurrences) but they had to be 'kept down'. In South Africa, this had to mean 'separate development' as apartheid was euphemistically called. Cricket was sadly used sometimes as the game of the conqueror, but not always. It became the game of the conquered in the West Indies, this perhaps explains my love of the West

Indians in summer 1963. In truth, there was a great deal to love there.

From now on, my summers were dictated by cricket. I started to play, but basically wasn't good enough. I could never really bat. I would get all the coaching books out of the local library and could tell everyone, geekishly and boringly, how to deal with the fast good-length ball just outside the off stump and how to read the spin bowler with all the quirks and shakes of his body and his arm to tell me how the ball was going to turn. I even knew how important it was to 'get to the pitch of the ball' – but when the ball came to me, I simply couldn't do it.

I worked hard at my bowling and eventually became a reasonable medium-pacer for my school team, and I was not a bad fielder. I had a problem (as did many boys) with being afraid of the hard ball – and had a few unhappy experiences of being hit – but I did have the advantage of being able to concentrate on every ball, something which very few of my peers seemed to have. I could be focussed on something, and no doubt if I have been a little younger and lived in the 2000s when such things became the fashion, somebody would have applied the label 'autistic' or 'on the spectrum' about me and my cricket.

Fielding was also something that I enjoyed. I modelled myself on Jackie McGlew and always played with my collar up as Jackie tended to do. I remembered how when he was fielding at mid-off, Jackie stopped a couple of fierce drives from Ted Dexter, possibly, or Colin Cowdrey, saving a four in each case, so he was my hero, even to the extent of me boring my friends with Brian Johnston's weak pun about 'glue on McGlew's fingers'.

But I preferred scoring. Now that was something that appealed to my geekish nature. The amount of leg byes conceded appeals to very few people indeed, but how I enjoyed that! The wicketkeeper could get annoyed when I started talking about byes, however!

And every summer was about the television and cricket. How I loved Richie Benaud – first as a player with 1961's Old Trafford Test etched in my mind, with a particular recollection of Brian Close's less happy and more self-destructive moments, and even my tender years were able to pick up the nuances of EW Swanton's commentary. The relationship between Close and Swanton in subsequent years was not a good one – in fact 'hate' is not too strong a word – and Swanton did not miss the stumps and hit the sightscreen about Close's manic, hysterical and short-lived innings that day. It was classic north v south stuff – outspoken, opinionated Yorkshireman v patrician, snobby, public school, *Daily Telegraph* writer, and, once I scratched the surface and wised up to the realities of life, Close and Swanton taught me an awful lot about the British class system as well!

1962 was a bit boring, but 1963 was a classic series against the West Indies. It was also the summer of the Profumo scandal and the great train robbery, with the Profumo scandal in particular causing me to realise that the Tories sometimes consorted with working-class girls (particularly one called Christine Keeler) in their spare time when I had been under the misapprehension that their entertainment was Lord's on a Saturday and the Church of England on a Sunday. But even that stunning realisation was not as important as the West Indies, and I recall our boys' cricket match grinding to a halt when someone arrived with a crackling transistor radio (a new symbol of working-class affluence) on the night that Colin

Cowdrey came out, his arm in plaster, to allow David Allen to bat out and England to earn a draw in that thrilling Lord's Test match.

And yet, the Profumo affair did have its effect on my cricket. 1963 was the year that I learned how to score – the start of another lifelong passion connected with the game. An over in which no runs are scored off the bat is called a maiden. I was able to work out the symbolism of why it was so called (nobody scored!) and enjoyed drawing the M in the scorebook. But if the bowler took a wicket as well, it was a W that you drew, and it was called a wicket maiden. Such was my precocious sense of humour that I called it a 'Christine Keeler'. Why? Because she was a 'wicked maiden'! I ignored the basic objections of the pedants that the word was wicket not wicked, and that Christine Keeler was no maiden. Indeed, if she had been, there would have been no problem, neither for Profumo nor anyone else! So, a wicket and five dots became a Christine Keeler, and if the bowler took another wicket it was a double wicket maiden and you could add Mandy Rice-Davies as well! Such outbursts of humour remained part of my repertoire for several years, until the more serious objection hit me and shamed me – namely that Christine and Mandy were in their own way victims of sexual abuse, and little more than playthings for men who were indeed 'wicked'.

But returning to 1960, why did South Africa lose? There is certainly no escaping the Griffin effect. Whatever one's feeling about Griffin and his action, there can be little doubt that South Africa handled it badly, not least in their half-heartedness about getting a replacement. On at least two, possibly three occasions, we were told that Heine was being sent for – but he never appeared. On at least two occasions, a South African-born fast bowler performed well for the opposition against the tourists and might have been asked to join the party. That never happened either. In addition, given that Griffin had been called for a no-ball in South Africa (admittedly not in the 1959/60 season) before he left their shores, why was he brought in the first place? Were there not other fast bowlers who might have done as well, if selected? As it was, the admirable Adcock had to struggle on with Jim Pothecary (a man who showed distinct improvement on the tour and indeed had his moments to boast about, but never quite ripped through the England batting) and the medium-paced Trevor Goddard – good, sound, reliable stuff, but again not quite what would have struck terror into the heart of the Englishmen.

And they could have played their best option in a wet summer – namely spin. They had the veteran Tayfield and the novice McKinnon. They were seldom, however, deployed at the same time. This was a shame, not least because it would have been the opposite of what England expected. The unexpected is often a great thing in cricket.

And in contrast to all this, was the England fast-bowling duo of Statham and Trueman. No one can exactly say when these two were at their peak, but it cannot have been far away from 1960. Statham the steady, good length, reliable hard worker who earned the lovely description by John Arlott of being 'so accurate that on soft turf the marks where he pitched were usually grouped like rifle shots round a bull's eye' and Trueman the fiery, frightening Freddie that he loved to be and to portray himself as, were a great pair to work in tandem, getting wickets for each other. Statham took 27 wickets, Trueman 25 and no other English bowler reached ten wickets in the series. Ray Illingworth was always a great favourite of mine but no great spinner emerged to replace Laker and Lock, and the reason was that there was no need. The Yorkshire and Lancashire duo did the job, helped by men like Alan Moss.

The South African batting was patchy with only one century in five Test matches. Waite was the best batsman, but it was McLean who got the century. McGlew disappointed in Test matches (he did better in the county matches) and none of the young batsmen like Carlstein, Wesley, Pithey or Fellows-Smith ever took a grip of a Test match and turned it round. And yet it remains an open question what would have happened if McLean had not suffered a 'rush of blood' to that dreadful long hop from Trueman in the second innings of the first Test match. South Africa might have won that Test match, and history would have been different.

For, in spite of all they tell you, words like 'momentum' and 'confidence' count for a great deal. It shouldn't happen, but professional cricketers do think they are 'meant to win' or 'meant to lose' on occasion, and their performances are consequently affected. There are often problems involved in playing 'what if', mainly in one's apparent lack of ability to restrain one's own imaginative powers, but if McLean had not been out early on that last day and South Africa had gone on to win, let us think what might have been.

McLean's own performances would have been a lot better, as indeed would have been the performances of some of the other, particularly the less experienced, batsmen. England might have panicked and changed their team more often. Success brings success and failure engenders more failure. One can recall England teams of the 1980s, for example, taking the field against the West Indies or in the 1990s facing the Australians. The Englishmen were already beaten in their hearts because the opposition were just too good – in the perception of the Englishmen. And yet they weren't necessarily invincible, if someone had just stood up to them. England in those days lacked what is now called 'mental toughness'.

As far as South Africa in 1960 were concerned, there was no more dismal surrender than at Trent Bridge in the first innings. Their total of 88 was pitiful. The bowling was good – but that was no surprise – but the resistance was feeble. They were then shamed into doing a little better in the follow-on, but they had defeated themselves mentally in the first innings.

And yet there was something that endeared the South Africans to me and indeed to the rest of the cricketing world. I suppose it could be called dignity. Their ability to take blows and knocks, some of them incredible and indeed virtually unprecedented, without apparently flinching was truly amazing. There was every opportunity for tantrums, spats and 'toys being thrown out of the pram' – but such behaviour never happened, at least not publicly. Neil Adcock was certainly an aggressive bowler, and one recalls with vivid clarity the look on his face at Trent Bridge that Saturday night in July which said that England were under no circumstances to get their required 49 runs that night. He certainly knew how to appeal aggressively as well, but there was never any bad behaviour when he didn't get his own way.

Umpires' decisions were always respected. South Africa, without any doubt, were on the wrong end of quite a few umpiring decisions. There is also more than a little evidence that umpires were under all sorts of political and journalistic pressure from time to time, and that they succumbed to it. The South Africans didn't make any fuss about this in public at the time. They did afterwards in books about the tour, and their own newspapers back home made a few perceptive points about what was happening, but there was never any protest or moaning about any decision. Even the crazy events of the exhibition match at Lord's were accepted with dignity.

All this was in distinct contrast to other occasions: like in 1973 when umpire Arthur Fagg refused to take the field one morning in protest against the West Indies' behaviour the night before after he had said 'not out'; or Mike Gatting and Shakoor Rana in Pakistan in 1987; or John Snow and Lou Rowan in Australia in 1971; or the worst of all when the Pakistan team refused to finish a Test match at The Oval in 2006 when the umpires thought that they might have been tampering with the ball.

There was no such kindergarten behaviour from the South Africans when many umpiring decisions went against them. Jackie McGlew certainly had no great tour himself with the bat, losing his wicket far too early on too many occasions, and at other times showing an unwarranted caution when he did not seem to realise that he had England where he wanted them, but in terms of discipline and behaviour, he led his team admirably from start to finish. He may have had his differences of opinion with the tour manager Dudley Nourse, but this was never obvious until afterwards, and frankly, he was a man who deserved better.

CHAPTER TEN

AND WHAT
HAPPENED TO THEM?

JACKIE McGLEW (1929–1998) CAPTAIN

Jackie McGlew disappeared from Test cricket soon after the 1960 tour. He played a couple of Test matches against New Zealand in 1961/62 and scored a century in one of them, but further trouble with his shoulder which had given him bother both before and during the 1960 tour compelled him to announce his retirement from Test match cricket. But he played on for Natal for about five years. He was always well-loved for his general enthusiasm for the game and deserves credit for his ability to instil in his players a love for fielding, an area of the game in which he himself always excelled.

He had always been a keen supporter of apartheid politics – something that was strange in view of his friendship with several Indian cricketers – and in 1969 agreed to stand as a candidate for the National Party in provincial elections. But he later withdrew for business reasons and never again involved himself in politics 'and retreated into religion' as his obituary in *Wisden 1999* put it.

He didn't retire from cricket altogether and was appointed manager of the first South African tour of the post-apartheid era, that of the under-19 team to the West Indies. This would seem to indicate a certain change of mind about apartheid and he was looked upon as a great success in the Caribbean.

He died of a blood disorder in Pretoria on 8 June 1998, aged 69.

TREVOR GODDARD (1931–2016) VICE-CAPTAIN

Trevor Goddard was an interesting character who became an evangelical preacher. It would have been interesting to know what his views on apartheid were. He certainly did a lot of unpaid work in the black townships in the later years of his life, and for that he deserves a great deal of respect, but it would have been nice to hear him denounce apartheid in 1960. He was certainly a great cricketer and in time would become a great captain.

Shortly after the end of the 1960 tour he announced his temporary retirement from Test match cricket and lived in London for a spell, believing that his son's bronchial condition would be better treated in Great Britain than anywhere else. But he returned to South Africa and was asked to lead the South African team to Australia in the 1963/64 season. He did well enough to earn a draw, although many people, including the Australians themselves, believed that he might have won the series if he had been a little bolder on occasion. He was kept on the following year to captain the South Africans for the visit of England in 1964/65. The English won 1-0 and Goddard, who had always led the side with dignity, quietly resigned.

On one occasion on this tour, England captain MJK Smith was given run out while 'gardening' when an over-zealous South African fielder threw down the wicket. This was the correct decision but Goddard withdrew the appeal and Smith was allowed to continue. This was in contrast to the incident at Trent Bridge in 1960 when McGlew was run out after an accidental collision and Cowdrey, although asking the umpires to change their decision, did not do what he technically should have done and withdraw the appeal.

At Johannesburg in the 1964/65 series, Goddard made his only Test match century. It will be recalled that he scored 99 at The Oval in 1960 before being caught by Cowdrey. Without making any too great a fuss about it, Goddard apparently believed that Cowdrey knew that he had not caught the ball cleanly. On this occasion in Johannesburg he was nearly run out on 99, when a throw-in by Tom Cartwright missed by a whisker!

He then retired from Test cricket again, but was once again prevailed upon to return for two series against Australia in 1966/67 and 1969/70. His dropping from the team was shabby. He had already said that he did not want to go to England in 1970, and once the series of 1969/70 was won, Goddard was told that he had been dropped for the final Test. It was a disappointing way to end his Test career, and extremely ironic in view of the fact that the 1970 tour never took place anyway!

He played in 41 Test matches and finished with a batting average of 34 and bowling average of 26, and is generally regarded as one of South Africa's greatest all-rounders. He also straddled several eras, having been in the Test team since 1955, and as captain and mentor deserved a great deal of credit for bringing on men like the Pollock brothers, Eddie Barlow and Colin Bland, all of whom acknowledged the part he played in their development.

In later years, in his largely unpaid works as an evangelical preacher, he worked with aspiring young South African sportsmen and effectively atoned for his apartheid past. Sadly, his wife Jean died of cancer in 1975, and he married his second wife Lesley a few years later. He survived a serious road accident in 1985 when he seemed to have fallen asleep at the wheel, and lived on for another 30 years until his death on 25 November 2016.

NEIL ADCOCK (1931–2013)

If Neil Adcock had had an opening partner as good as he himself was in 1960, the outcome would have been a great deal different. As it was, Adcock was good enough to be chosen as one of the five Cricketers of the Year in

Wisden 1961, and was the only overseas fast bowler to have taken more than 100 wickets on the tour. Sadly, Griffin's action was suspect, Jim Pothecary was just a trifle inexperienced and for reasons best known to themselves, the South Africans failed to summon Peter Heine to help Adcock. At the prime of his abilities, Neil (sometimes called NAT because of the initials for Neil Amwin Treharne) bowled well throughout, keeping a better control of line and length than he had done on a few previous occasions.

He was apparently very relieved that he saw the tour out without breaking down and, after playing in the 1961/62 series against New Zealand, he retired from Test match cricket, having taken 104 wickets at an average of 21 in 26 matches. In domestic cricket he played for both Natal and Transvaal, and is generally regarded as having been one of the fastest South African bowlers of them all. In later years he became a radio commentator and was very highly regarded in that job as well. He died in Howick, South Africa on 6 January 2013 at the age of 81.

PETER CARLSTEIN (1938–)

Peter played a total of eight Test matches for South Africa but when he was in New Zealand in February 1964 he received the devastating news that his wife and children had been killed in a road accident. He played on for a good few years, but then he moved to Perth in Western Australia after his first-class career finished. He was well known as a feisty character, and on one famous occasion when playing for Rhodesia/Zimbabwe thrust the handle of his bat into a wicketkeeper's chest after being provoked by some odd 'sledging' which included the silent treatment.

CHRIS DUCKWORTH (1933–2014)

The deputy wicketkeeper who had also toured in that capacity in 1955, he never played a Test match in England but did play twice when South Africa hosted England in 1956/57. He was a Rhodesian, who was also an international at hockey, and played rugby for Natal. He did not play much cricket but he did turn out for the Wanderers in season 1965/66. He died aged 81 on 16 May 2014.

JONATHAN FELLOWS-SMITH
(1932–2013)

Nicknamed 'Pom Pom' for some unfathomable reason on the tour, he did not play much cricket after this, and indeed lived most of the rest of his life in England. He died on 28 September 2013 in the Luton and Dunstable Hospital, at the age of 81. He was chosen for this tour because of his knowledge of English conditions, having played for Northants.

He is one of the few tourists who seemed to have some obvious disapproval of apartheid, for he was a keen supporter of Basil D'Oliveira, and wrote an article in *The Cricketer* magazine in 1961 in which he stated that: 'If the game can conceivably be used as a force to unite conflicting racial groups, there seems to be no reason why South African cricket should not recover from its present malaise.' Such an opinion seems to have been considered treason in South Africa at the time, and he was never again considered for the Test match team. In truth, he probably was not a Test match player, but he was good enough at a slightly lower level and also distinguished himself at rugby and tennis.

GEOFF GRIFFIN (1939–2006)

The tragic hero of this tour lived a quiet life after this trauma. He played only a few more games of cricket, and never at Test level. To his intense credit he resisted any 'chequebook journalism' attempts to make money, and contented himself by running a couple of hotels in Rhodesia. Famously gracious and forgiving about the whole business, he died tragically and suddenly on 16 November 2006 while speaking to his old school, Durban High School. He was a much-loved and respected figure, and history remains divided about the events of 1960, although the 'political' dimension to it all can scarcely be denied.

It is generally agreed that he had a strange action brought about by a childhood accident, but one would also have to be very naïve to ignore the strong whiff of a conspiracy in order for England to 'choose' the Australian team for the following summer. Even some South African journalists think that he was a 'chucker' but others like Australian journalists and even ex-England batsman Denis Compton were not quite so sure. What is certainly true is that Griffin was more or less the only person in the whole business who acted with dignity and respect. And he remains the first man to have taken a hat-trick in a Test match at Lord's.

ATHOLL McKINNON (1932–1983)

A protégé of the great 'Tufty' Mann, Atholl McKinnon died suddenly in Durban at the age of 51 on 2 December 1983 when he was, ironically enough, acting as manager of an unofficial West Indies side which was touring South Africa.

He was the first of the 1960 side to die, and he was much missed because he was a popular character. He was the only member of the 1960 side who returned for the next visit in 1965, a spectacular half-tour which was as successful as the 1960 tour had been disappointing. He played in the last two Test matches of 1965 without doing very much but his best Test match had been at Johannesburg earlier in the year when he took seven wickets in the match, but neither he nor anyone else could dislodge Geoff Boycott. He also played a part in the victory over Australia in 1966/67. In all, he took 26 wickets at 35.57 each.

ROY McLEAN (1930–2007)

In some ways the odd man out of this tour, Roy McLean had the honour of being chosen one as one of the five Cricketers of the Year in *Wisden 1961* and, among other complimentary things, he was described as 'the lone representative of attacking batsmanship', something that one feels is a bit hard on the other members of the side. He came back to England the following year in 1961 as captain and leader of an unofficial team of South African youngsters called the Fezelas, containing men like Peter Pollock, Colin Bland and Eddie Barlow, and the successful South African side of the mid 1960s owes a lot to the experience gained in English conditions under the wise leadership of Roy McLean. His own Test career failed to thrive after that. He did score a century against New Zealand in 1961/62 but missed the Australian tour in 1963/64 and played only twice against England in 1964/65, both times batting at number six, which did not suit him.

He announced his retirement from Test cricket after that and did not play very much cricket at all, other than a couple of games for Natal. He became an insurance

275

salesman, led a quiet family life, and died in Johannesburg on 26 August 2007 at the age of 77.

SID O'LINN (1927–2016)

This interesting character died in obscurity on 11 December 2016 at the age of 89. The story of him changing his name to play down his Jewish background has been told in another chapter of this book, but *Wisden 2017* also tells a fascinating story about how he rushed through his divorce from his wife before coming to England in 1960. His wife still lived in England and he was afraid of running into her! He had of course played for Kent and Charlton Athletic, and although he played well for Kent, he was not re-engaged after 1952, the reason apparently being that he did not like having to call the amateurs 'Mister'. It is a shame, therefore, that his apparent socialism and decency in other aspects of his life, as well as his obvious fear of persecution for being Jewish, did not impel him to question apartheid a little oftener and a little more volubly! He played another two Test matches for South Africa against New Zealand in season 1961/62 but without any great success, and he quietly disappeared from the scene.

In later years he ran a sports shop in Johannesburg along with wicketkeeper John Waite. He himself had been a wicketkeeper in his years with Kent. He is one of the few people (possibly the only one) to have played for South Africa at both football and cricket. His 98 at Trent Bridge in July 1960 remains the highlight of his cricketing career.

ANTHONY PITHEY (1933–2006)

Tony Pithey did not have a great tour in 1960, suffering from back problems and the sort of 'virus' issues which affect quite a few tourists in a foreign country, and one never knows whether they are the cause or the effect of poor on-field performances. But he was generally regarded as a solid batsman with fine technique against fast bowling in particular, but he was never really an aggressive batsman, a fault that had been laid at the door of several South African batsmen of that era. He did tolerably well against Australia in 1963/4 and in the attritional series against England in season 1964/65. He scored a century in that series at Newlands and was considered good enough to be selected for the tour of England in 1965, but he declined for business reasons and returned to his native Rhodesia.

His brother David also played for South Africa, several times in the same side as Tony. The contrast between the dour, technically correct but dull Pithey brothers on the one hand and the flamboyant Pollocks on the other was much commented upon. Tony played 17 Test matches for South Africa and died on 17 November 2006.

JIM POTHECARY (1933–2016)

The 1960 tour marked the end of Jim Pothecary's Test match career, and he played only a few more games for Western Province. He was called on to do a difficult job in covering for Geoff Griffin, and he was certainly beginning to show some improvement. *Wisden*'s assessment of him being 'probably the biggest disappointment' of the 1960 tour seems harsh, although he certainly did not bowl well at The Oval when England rescued themselves from a losing position, and when South Africa needed a good performance. He died in Cape Town on 11 May 2016.

HUGH TAYFIELD (1929–1994)

Hugh 'Toey' Tayfield died in hospital in Durban on 25 February 1994. He was called 'Toey' because of his habit of stubbing his toe into the ground as he bowled. He was recognised as one of the best spin bowlers that South Africa had ever produced, and was particularly renowned for his ability to keep hitting the spot, over after over. He had been a fine bowler for South Africa (he certainly had his moments in 1955 and 1956/57) but the 1960 tour represented his swansong. He did not do well in Test matches although his haul against the counties was considerable. He was not the worst batsman in the world either. In his private life, he married and divorced five times. Even in a profession which is hardly renowned for its marital constancy or sexual fidelity, this is a little on the extreme side, and jokes were often made as he handed over his cap to the umpire and kissed the badge (as was his wont) that things would not have been so bad if he had stuck to kissing the badge. In later years he also had problems in business. He had been ill for a long time before his death in 1994.

JOHN WAITE (1930–2011)

A curious, complex but always interesting character, John Waite died in Johannesburg on 22 June 2011 at the age of 81. He was an outstanding wicketkeeper and a solid batsman. He was not without his arguments and quarrels with his team-mates, but was renowned for his gentlemanly behaviour on the field. He was also renowned for his ability to be run out, however! He played on until the 1964/65 series against England.

His book *Perchance to Bowl*, written in tandem with a strange character with the equally unlikely name of Dick Whitington, was controversial to say the least. It is certainly well worth a read for he describes the 1960 tour in a jaunty and always entertaining sort of style, combining details of the play with insight and inside information. But it is the other part of the book and what he says about apartheid that is interesting, albeit a little depressing, some 60 years down the line. One would like to think that much of the book was written tongue in cheek, but one has the nasty suspicion that it was not. And yet, in other respects, he comes across as far too intelligent a man to believe what he was saying.

To his credit, in later life he involved himself as an administrator in Gauteng cricket when Transvaal became Gauteng, and he worked very hard in the multiracial development of the sport. He also, late in life, conceded that Griffin did throw, but he had the tact to wait until Griffin was dead before saying so.

COLIN WESLEY (1937–)

'Tich' never really recovered from his infamous 'king pair' at Trent Bridge as far as Test match cricket was concerned, for he never played Test match cricket again, although he did play a few games for Natal. He now owns a chain of tobacco stores in South Africa.

STATISTICS

N.B. To be perfectly accurate 'South Africa' means the team in a Test match, while 'the South Africans' means the tourists in all games.

SOUTH AFRICA TEST MATCHES BATTING

	Innings	Not Out	Runs	Highest Score	Average
JHB Waite	9	2	267	77	38.14
RA McLean	9	1	269	109	33.62
S O'Linn	8	0	261	98	32.62
JP Fellows-Smith	8	2	166	35	27.66
TL Goddard	10	1	220	99	24.44
DJ McGlew	10	1	189	45	21.00
PR Carlstein	9	0	119	42	13.22
HJ Tayfield	8	1	92	46*	13.14

AJ Pithey	3	0	30	17	10.00
C Wesley	5	0	49	35	9.80
JE Pothecary	4	0	26	12	6.50
G Griffin	4	0	25	14	6.25
NAT Adcock	8	4	20	8*	5.00

Also batted: AH McKinnon 22

SOUTH AFRICA TEST MATCHES BOWLING

	Overs	Maidens	Runs	Wickets	Average
NAT Adcock	263	69	587	26	22.57
G Griffin	72	14	192	8	24.00
TL Goddard	202	79	414	17	24.35
AH McKinnon	26	8	64	2	32.00
HJ Tayfield	186.3	68	454	12	37.83
JE Pothecary	138	32	354	9	39.33
JP Fellows-Smith	19	1	61	0	-

ENGLAND TEST MATCHES BATTING

	Innings	Not Out	Runs	Highest Score	Average
G Pullar	6	1	293	175	58.60
R Subba Row	6	1	251	90	50.20
KF Barrington	7	1	227	80	37.83

MC Cowdrey	9	0	312	155	34.66
MJK Smith	6	0	192	99	32.00
PM Walker	4	0	128	52	32.00
ER Dexter	9	0	241	56	26.77
R Illingworth	6	2	81	37	20.25
JM Parks	8	0	154	36	19.25
JB Statham	7	3	57	22	14.25
FS Trueman	8	1	99	25	14.14
DA Allen	4	2	26	14*	13.00
DEV Padgett	4	0	51	31	12.73

Also batted: RW Barber 5 and 4; T Greenhough 2; AE Moss 3*

ENGLAND TEST MATCHES BOWLING

	Overs	*Maidens*	*Runs*	*Wickets*	*Average*
AE Moss	50.1	7	138	9	15.33
JB Statham	203	54	491	27	18.18
FS Trueman	180.3	31	508	25	20.32
R Illingworth	77	32	146	6	24.33
DA Allen	56.5	26	101	4	25.25
ER Dexter	64.2	16	157	5	31.40
T Greenhough	49	19	102	2	51.00

RW Barber	16	2	55	1	55.00
PM Walker	13	3	34	0	-
KF Barrington	3	1	5	0	-
MC Cowdrey	1	0	4	0	-
DEV Padgett	2	0	8	0	-
G Pullar	1	0	6	0	-

THE SOUTH AFRICANS TOUR AVERAGES BATTING

	Matches	Innings	Not Out	Runs	Highest Score	Average
DJ McGlew	25	39	8	1327	151*	42.80
RA McLean	26	43	3	1516	207	37.90
TL Goddard	24	39	2	1377	186*	37.21
S O'Linn	24	37	9	1014	120*	36.21
JHB Waite	24	31	6	894	125	35.76
JP Fellows-Smith	23	34	7	863	109*	31.96
PR Carlstein	24	39	6	980	151	29.69
AJ Pithey	18	25	3	614	96	27.90
C Wesley	21	31	4	595	90	22.03
CAR Duckworth	18	25	2	426	59	18.52
G Griffin	18	22	2	353	65*	17.65
JE Pothecary	21	24	4	277	68	13.85

HJ Tayfield	26	31	7	315	46*	13.12
AH McKinnon	18	14	6	70	22	8.75
NAT Adcock	20	20	5	71	11	4.73

THE SOUTH AFRICANS TOUR
AVERAGES BOWLING

	Overs	Maidens	Runs	Wickets	Average
NAT Adcock	737	196	1515	108	14.02
TL Goddard	752.2	308	1439	73	19.71
AH McKinnon	436.1	136	1107	53	20.88
HJ Tayfield	1048	333	2664	123	21.65
G Griffin	259.4	71	612	26	23.53
JP Fellows-Smith	319.4	69	829	32	25.90
JE Pothecary	632.5	163	1565	53	29.52
DJ McGlew	75.1	13	264	8	33.00
PR Carlstein	36.2	3	158	4	39.50

Also bowled: RA McLean 9.2 0 28 2; JHB Waite 1 0 1
0; C Wesley 15 3 51 4

THE SOUTH AFRICANS TOUR FIELDING

	Catches	Stumpings
JHB Waite	54	9
TL Goddard	26	
CAR Duckworth	22	2
RA McLean	22	
JP Fellows-Smith	19	
HJ Tayfield	19	
S O'Linn	18	
JE Pothecary	18	
PR Carlstein	12	
DJ McGlew	12	
AJ Pithey	10	
C Wesley	8	
NAT Adcock	7	
G Griffin	6	
AH McKinnon	1	

Victories – Worcestershire, Derbyshire, Essex, Cambridge University, Minor Counties, Glamorgan (twice), Somerset, Hampshire, Kent, Combined Services, AER Gilligan's XI, a Lancashire XI, TN Pearce's XI

Draws – England (twice), Oxford University, MCC, Nottinghamshire, Lancashire, Leicestershire, Middlesex, Surrey, Warwickshire, Yorkshire

Abandoned – Sussex

Defeats – England (three times), Northamptonshire, Gloucestershire

Also available at all good book stores

9781785316395

9781785317224

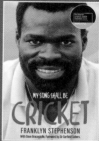

9781785315398

9781785319860

9781785318412

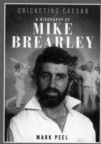

9781785316623

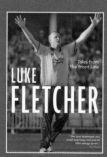

9781785316876

9781785318405

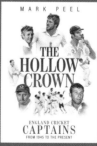

9781785316630